Managing
Conflict
Resolution

Character Education

Character Education

Managing Conflict Resolution

SEAN McCOLLUM

CONSULTING EDITORS AND INTRODUCTION BY
Madonna M. Murphy, Ph.D
University of St. Francis
and ### Sharon L. Banas
former Values Education Coordinator,
Sweet Home Central School District, New York

CHELSEA HOUSE
PUBLISHERS
An imprint of Infobase Publishing

Chelsea House
An imprint of Infobase Publishing
132 West 31st Street
New York NY 10001

Library of Congress Cataloging-in-Publication Data
McCollum, Sean.
  Managing conflict resolution / Sean McCollum.
     p. cm. — (Character education)
  Includes bibliographical references and index.
  ISBN 978-1-60413-122-2 (hardcover)
  1. Conflict management—United States—Juvenile literature. 2. Social conflict—United States—Juvenile literature. 3. Conflict (Psychology)—Juvenile literature. I. Title. II. Series.

  HM1126.M393 2009
  303.6'90973—dc22   2009001086

Chelsea House books are available at special discounts when purchased in bulk quantities for businesses, associations, institutions, or sales promotions. Please call our Special Sales Department in New York at (212) 967-8800 or (800) 322-8755.

You can find Chelsea House on the World Wide Web
at http://www.chelseahouse.com

Text design by Annie O'Donnell
Cover design by Takeshi Takahashi

Printed in the United States

Bang EJB 10 9 8 7 6 5 4 3 2 1

This book is printed on acid-free paper.

All links and Web addresses were checked and verified to be correct at the time of publication. Because of the dynamic nature of the Web, some addresses and links may have changed since publication and may no longer be valid.

CONTENTS

INTRODUCTION

O n February 14, 2008, as these books were being edited, a shooting occurred at Northern Illinois University (NIU) in DeKalb, Illinois. A former NIU graduate student, dressed in black and armed with a shotgun and two handguns, opened fire from the stage of a lecture hall. The shooter killed five students and injured 16 others before committing suicide. What could have led someone to do this? Could it have been prevented?

When the shooting started, student Dan Parmenter and his girlfriend, Lauren Debrauwere, who was sitting next to him, dropped to the floor between the rows of seats. Dan covered Lauren with his body, held her hand, and began praying. The shield of Dan's body saved Lauren's life, but Dan was fatally wounded. In that hall, on February 14, 2008—Valentine's Day—one person's deed was horrific and filled with hate; another's was heroic and loving.

The purpose of this series of books is to help prevent the occurrence of this kind of violence by offering readers the character education and social and emotional skills they need to control their emotions and make good moral choices. This series includes books on topics such as coping with bullying, conflicts, peer pressure, prejudice, anger and frustration, and numerous responsibilities, as well as learning how to handle teamwork and respect for others, be fair and honest, and be a good leader and decision-maker.

In his 1992 book, *Why Johnny Can't Tell Right from Wrong*,[1] William Kilpatrick coined the term "moral illiteracy" and dedicated a whole chapter to it. Today, as he points out, people often do not recognize when they are in a situation that calls for a moral choice, and they are not able to define what is right and what is wrong in that situation. The California-based Josephson Institute of Ethics agrees with these concerns. The institute states that we have a "character deficit" in our society today and points out that increasing numbers of young people across the United States—from well-to-do as well as disadvantaged backgrounds—demonstrate reckless disregard for fundamental standards of ethical conduct.

According to the 2006 *Josephson Institute Report Card on the Ethics of American Youth*, our children are at risk. This report sets forth the results of a biannual written survey completed in 2006 by more than 36,000 high school students across the country. The compilers of the report found that 82 percent of the students surveyed admitted that they had lied to a parent about something significant within the previous year. Sixty percent admitted to having cheated during a test at school, and 28 percent admitted to having stolen something from a store.[2] (Various books in this series will tell of other findings in this report.) Clearly, helping young people to develop character is a need of national importance.

The United States Congress agrees. In 1994, in the joint resolution that established National Character Counts Week, Congress declared that "the character of a nation is only as strong as the character of its individual citizens." The resolution also stated that "people do not automatically develop good character and, therefore, conscientious efforts must be made by youth-influencing institutions . . . to help young people develop the essential traits and characteristics that comprise good character."[3]

Many stories can be told of people who have defended our nation with character. One of the editors of this series knew one such young man named Jason Dunham. On April 24, 2004, Corporal Jason L. Dunham was serving with the United States Marines in Iraq. As Corporal Dunham's squad was conducting a reconnaissance mission, the men heard sounds of rocket-propelled grenades and small arms fire. Corporal

Dunham led a team of men toward that fire to assist their battalion commander's ambushed convoy. An insurgent leaped out at Corporal Dunham, and he saw the man release a grenade. Corporal Dunham alerted his team and immediately covered the grenade with his helmet and his body. He lost his own life, but he saved the lives of others on his team.

In January 2007, the Dunham family traveled to Washington, D.C., where President George W. Bush presented them with Corporal Dunham's posthumously awarded Congressional Medal of Honor. In the words of the Medal of Honor citation, "By his undaunted courage, intrepid fighting spirit, and unwavering devotion to duty, Corporal Dunham gallantly gave his life for his country."[4]

Thomas Lickona, the author of several books including *Educating for Character* and *Character Matters*, explains that the premise of character education is that there are objectively good human qualities—virtues—that are enduring moral truths. Courage, fortitude, integrity, caring, citizenship, and trustworthiness are just a few examples. These moral truths transcend religious, cultural, and social differences and help us to distinguish right from wrong. They are rooted in our human nature. They tell us how we should act with other human beings to promote human dignity and build a well-functioning and civil society—a society in which everyone lives by the golden rule.[5]

To develop his or her character, a person must understand core virtues, care about them, and act upon them. This series of books aims to help young readers *want* to become people of character. The books will help young people understand such core ethical values as fairness, honesty, responsibility, respect, tolerance of others, fortitude, self-discipline, teamwork, and leadership. By offering examples of people today and notable figures in history who live and have lived these virtues, these books will inspire young readers to develop these traits in themselves.

Finally, through these books, young readers will see that if they act on these moral truths, they will make good choices.

They will be able to deal with frustration and anger, manage conflict resolution, overcome prejudice, handle peer pressure, and deal with bullying. The result, one hopes, will be middle schools, high schools, and neighborhoods in which young people care about one another and work with their class-mates and neighbors to develop team spirit.

Character development is a lifelong task but an exciting challenge. The need for it has been with us since the begin-ning of civilization. As the ancient Greek philosopher Aristo-tle explained in his *Nicomachean Ethics*:

> The virtues we get by first exercising them . . . so too we become just by doing just acts, temperate by doing tem-perate acts, brave by doing brave acts. . . . Hence also it is no easy task to be good . . . to do this to the right person, to the right extent, at the right time, with the right motive, and in the right way, that is not easy; wherefore goodness is both rare and laudable and noble. . . . It makes no small difference, then, whether we form habits of one kind or of another from our very youth; it makes a very great differ-ence, or rather all the difference.[6]

This development of one's character is truly *The Ultimate Gift* that we hope to give to our young people. In the movie version of Jim Stovall's book of the same name, a privileged young man receives a most unexpected inheritance from his grandfather. Instead of the sizeable inheritance of cash that he expects, the young man receives 12 tasks—or "gifts"—designed to challenge him on a journey of self-discovery. The gifts confront him with character choices that force him to decide how one can be truly happy. Is it the possession of money that brings us happiness, or is it what we do with the money that we have? Every one of us has been given gifts. Will we keep our gifts to ourselves, or will we share them with others?

Being a "person of character" can have multiple meanings. Psychologist Steven Pinker asks an interesting question in a

January 13, 2008, *New York Times Magazine* article titled "The Moral Instinct": "Which of the following people would you say is the most admirable: Mother Teresa, Bill Gates, or Norman Borlaug?" Pinker goes on to explain that although most people would say that, of course, Mother Teresa is the most admirable—a true person of character who ministered to the poor in Calcutta, was awarded the Noble Peace Prize, and was ranked in an American poll as the most admired person in the twentieth century—each of these three is a morally admirable person.

Pinker points out that Bill Gates made billions through his company Microsoft, but he also has decided to give away billions of dollars to help alleviate human misery in the United States and around the world. His charitable foundation is built on the principles that "All lives—no matter where they are being lived—have equal value" and "To whom much is given, much is expected."

Pinker notes that very few people have heard of Norman Borlaug, an agronomist who has spent his life developing high-yielding varieties of crops for third world countries. He is known as the "Father of the Green Revolution" because he used agricultural science to reduce world hunger and, by doing so, saved more than a billion lives. Borlaug is one of only five people in history to have won the Nobel Peace Prize, the Presidential Medal of Freedom, and the Congressional Gold Medal. He has devoted his long professional life and his scientific expertise to making the world a better place.

All of these people—although very different, from different places, and with different gifts—are people of character. They are, says Pinker, people with "a sixth sense, the moral sense." It is the sense of trying to do good in whatever situation one finds oneself.[7]

The authors and editors of the series *Character Education* hope that these books will help young readers discover their gifts and develop them, guided by a moral compass. "Do good and avoid evil." "Become all that you can be—a person of character." The books in this series teach these things and more. These books will correlate well with national social studies standards of learning. They will help teachers meet state standards for teaching social and emotional skills, as well as state guidelines for teaching ethics and character education.

Madonna M. Murphy, Ph.D.
Author of *Character Education in America's Blue Ribbon Schools* and professor of education, University of St. Francis, Joliet, Illinois

Sharon L. Banas, M.Ed.
Author of *Caring Messages for the School Year* and former character education coordinator and middle school social studies teacher, Sweet Home Central School District, Amherst and Tonawanda, New York

FOOTNOTES
1. William Kilpatrick. *Why Johnny Can't Tell Right from Wrong*, New York: Simon and Schuster, 1992.
2. Josephson Institute, 2006 *Josephson Institute Report Card on the Ethics of American Youth: Part One – Integrity*. Available online at: http://josephsoninstitute.org/pdf/ReportCard_press-release_2006-1013.pdf.
3. House Joint Resolution 366. May 11, 1994, 103rd Congress. 2d Session.
4. U.S. Army Center of Military History. *The Medal of Honor*. Available online at: www.history.army.mil/moh.html.
5. Thomas Lickona, *Educating for Character: Teaching Respect and Responsibility in the Schools*. New York: Bantam, 1991. Thomas Lickona, *Character Matters: How to Help Our Children Develop Good Judgment, Integrity, and Other Essential Virtues*. New York: Simon and Schuster Touchstone Books, 2004.
6. Richard McKeon, editor, "Nicomachean Ethics." *Basic Works of Aristotle*, Chicago: Random House, Clarendon Press, 1941.
7. Steven Pinker, "The Moral Instinct," *The New York Times*, January 13, 2008. Available online at www.newyorktimes.com.

THE MANY FORMS OF CONFLICT

Peace is not the absence of conflict but the presence of creative alternatives for responding to conflict.

—Dorothy Thompson (1893–1961), U.S. journalist

The photographs showed trouble. A U.S. spy plane had flown over the island country of Cuba and spotted missile sites under construction. The Soviet Union (present-day Russia) was helping Cuba install missile bases less than 100 miles from Florida. From there, the Soviets would be able to strike U.S. cities with nuclear weapons within minutes of launch. U.S. President John F. Kennedy quickly called a meeting of his top advisers.

This event, known as the Cuban Missile Crisis, was part of the Cold War. The Cold War was a struggle between the Soviet Union and the United States for power in the world. For 13 days in October 1962, however, this "cold" conflict threatened to turn very, very "hot." The world teetered on the edge of a devastating war. The outcome would depend on the conflict resolution skills of the leaders of the two sides.

President John F. Kennedy (*right*) sits with (*from left*) General David Shoup, Marine Corps Commandant, and Admiral George Anderson, Chief of U.S. Naval Operations, in 1962 to discuss Cuba and the operation of the U.S. naval blockade.

CONFLICT IS A FACT OF LIFE

Conflicts happen, whether in a family argument or an international face-off such as the Cuban Missile Crisis. No matter how people might try to avoid butting heads with others, sooner or later a situation comes along that cannot be dodged. People often create conflicts as they pursue what they want and need. How individuals handle such disputes reveals a lot about their character, and helps develop character as well.

Conflict plays a role in every circle of human society: within families and communities, between groups, and among nations. The Mediation Center at El Centro College in Dallas,

Texas, defines *conflict* as "behavior in which people oppose one another in their thoughts, feelings, and/or actions." For some people, the term *conflict* may bring up images of protest marches or battle scenes. For others, it might bring memories of a playground scuffle or hurt feelings from a friend's gossip. Perhaps *conflict* brings to mind a parent, coach, or teacher challenging a young person to do better or try harder. All of these situations are examples of conflict.

When people encounter conflict, it can be upsetting and even scary. Conflicts can become destructive if they slide into abuse, rage, or violence. If handled properly, however, they can also cause new growth and development. They can inspire individuals, communities, and nations to find courage and strength that they did not know they had. A confrontation can stop abuse and injustice. Conflict can also lead to cooperation and the quest for creative solutions. In his 1996 book, *Conflict Resolution: Theory, Research, and Practice,* James Schellenberg, an expert on relationships among people and cultures, explained:

> Conflict is so fully a part of all forms of society that we should appreciate its importance—for stimulating new thoughts, for promoting social change, for defining our group relationships, for helping us form our senses of personal identity, and for many other things we take for granted in our everyday lives. . . . The things we love, as well as those we despise are . . . shaped by social conflict.

At the root of all conflicts are what psychologist Abraham Maslow called "unmet needs." These needs may be physical ones, such as food, water, shelter, and safety. Unmet needs may also be psychological—related to thoughts, beliefs, and emotions. Psychological needs fall into four main areas:

❀ Relationships: the need to belong and work together, to be respected, and to love and be loved

* Capability: the need to set goals, achieve, and receive recognition for achieving
* Independence: the need to make one's own choices and decisions
* Pleasure: the need to have fun and enjoy life

In any conflict, a useful question to ask is "What are the unmet needs here?" Whatever they are, they will most likely need to be addressed before the dispute will end.

Because conflict is a regular part of life, it makes sense that people have developed methods for dealing with it and

Coach Vince Lombardi (*left*) of the Green Bay Packers relaxes with friend and rival Wellington Mara, co-owner of the New York Giants, in 1962 in Rome. Lombardi knew how to use conflict in a healthy way—to promote teamwork and toughness on the field.

for using conflict to do good things. For example, talented coaches and teachers know how to use conflict to motivate players and students to achieve. Vince Lombardi, the legendary head coach of the Green Bay Packers football team, was known for being a genius at getting the most out of his football team. He used a combination of enthusiastic encouragement and fierce, but constructive, criticism. "Lombardi treated us all the same, like dogs," joked Hall of Fame member Jerry Kramer, a Packers offensive lineman. The coach also "made us all better than we thought we could be," Kramer added.

It is possible to learn the skills needed to manage conflict and conflict resolution. Like any skills, these ones require practice. People who struggle to resolve conflicts have a disadvantage as they face the world. They are more likely to react to a dispute without thinking clearly. They may get upset, run away, or throw a punch if a situation gets tense.

In contrast, people who learn to cope well with conflict demonstrate what writer Ernest Hemingway called "grace under pressure." That is the ability to stay calm, cool, and logical when facing a challenge. People who develop good conflict resolution skills also exercise all four of the "essential virtues" noted by the philosophers of ancient Greece: wisdom, justice, fortitude, and self-control. Nurturing these abilities can only serve to make people—and the world—better, happier, and safer.

DESTRUCTIVE CONFLICT

Finding destructive conflict in the world is very easy: The public is bombarded with news of war and violent crime. Heroes and villains in blockbuster movies rarely settle matters without bullets flying, buildings exploding, and people dying. Gossip blogs blare headlines about bitter celebrity divorces and fights.

METHODS FOR MANAGING CONFLICT

Conflicts can be managed in a number of ways. Some strategies, such as negotiation, involve direct discussions between the different sides in a dispute. Other methods may include help from outside parties not directly involved in the conflict. Some of the following approaches may help resolve a conflict, while others will make it worse.

Avoidance: A person might use this strategy to steer clear of conflict, for any number of reasons. He or she may decide that a confrontation will prove more trouble than it is worth. For example, the other side may have too much strength or authority to face. The avoider might also, however, lack the confidence to deal with the conflict directly.

Independent action: This approach involves one side starting a conflict with little or no effort to communicate with the other side. It often involves violence, illegal acts, or both. A robbery or brawl might be an example of this. Independent action is almost always a bad idea.

When conflict arises, it has the potential to become either a destructive or constructive situation. According to conflict resolution expert Morton Deutsch, the direction it takes depends on many factors. These include the history behind the dispute, what is at stake, and the values and emotions connected to it. The outcome is also influenced by the attitudes, conflict resolution skills, and experience of the people in the conflict. When the people lack experience in conflict resolution, there is a greater chance that the dispute will turn destructive.

Four traits often mark destructive conflict. The first is miscommunication, when a message a person is trying to communicate is not the message the other side

Negotiation: Negotiation consists of the different sides talking one-on-one to try to work out a resolution.

Mediation: This strategy is similar to negotiation. The difference is that an outside party—a mediator—takes part. The mediator makes no decisions, but helps smooth communication between the sides of the conflict. The mediator also referees discussions so that they remain fair and respectful.

Arbitration: Like mediation, arbitration involves an outside party taking part in discussions. An arbitrator is a person who may assist by listening, refereeing, and asking questions. In this case, though, the arbitrator makes a judgment about how the conflict should be resolved. Before starting arbitration, opposing sides must agree to follow the arbitrator's decision.

Litigation: The use of the legal system to settle a dispute is called litigation. A lawsuit may be settled in negotiations between lawyers. The suit may also go to court where a legal decision may be handed down by a judge or jury.

understands. Distrust and strong emotions can contribute to these misunderstandings.

The second trait is called "kitchen sinking." That term comes from the phrase "everything but the kitchen sink," meaning that people throw all sorts of unrelated frustrations into the specific conflict. For example, a mother might get angry at her teen for not taking out the garbage. If the teen talks back rudely, the mother may start complaining about other mistakes the teen has made. Kitchen sinking usually occurs when resentments have built up between people or groups.

The third trait is the demonizing of the other side—when one side accuses the other side of evil motives in the conflict.

These accusations are likely to cause the destructive conflict to worsen. Demonizing enemies is a common action in wartime.

Lastly, a feature of many destructive conflicts is the desire to win completely. This may be acceptable and exciting in sports, but it can prove disastrous in other areas. If the winning side humiliates the losing side, it may cause feelings of resentment and hatred. This can easily sabotage any resolution and may keep the conflict alive for years—even for generations.

In the mid 1800s, all four of these traits emerged in the conflict between white settlers and Native American tribes of the Great Plains. In the 1860s, a growing number of whites wanted much of this land for their farms and towns. Not surprisingly, the Lakota, Dakota, Cheyenne, and other native peoples who already lived there opposed them.

U.S. officials promised the Native Americans control of all land in the Dakota Territory. "No white person or persons shall be permitted to settle upon or occupy any portion of the territory, or without the consent of the Indians to pass through the same," ordered the Laramie Treaty of 1868. That promise was soon broken. U.S. soldiers arrived to build forts and carve out trails. This led to attacks by the Native Americans, counterattacks by U.S. troops, and then war. Attitudes in the white press painted the Native Americans as "wild savages." In 1869, U.S. General Philip Sheridan was quoted as saying, "The only good Indians I ever saw were dead."

The conflict took a turn for the worse in 1874. Gold was found in the Black Hills region of South Dakota. The Black Hills are holy to the Plains tribes in that area. White prospectors flocked to the region to strike it rich. Conflict between the Native Americans and gold seekers heated up.

U.S. soldiers at first tried to keep the prospectors out, as the U.S. government had promised leaders of the Plains tribes. They failed. The government canceled the order, and abandoned efforts to respect the wants and needs of the

In 1875, a delegation of Sioux leaders traveled to Washington, D.C., to protest the government's violation of the Fort Laramie Treaty of 1868. They were frustrated by the dwindling size of their reservation and a decrease in their food supply.

native people there. Army troops were sent out to crush Native American resistance once and for all. Within 16 years, they had all but succeeded. Survivors of the Plains tribes were forced onto reservations.

More than a century has passed since the end of this conflict, but its outcome still haunts relations between white Americans and Native Americans who live in the Great Plains region. Destructive conflict almost always leaves bitterness as its legacy.

CONSTRUCTIVE CONFLICT

In contrast to destructive conflict, constructive conflict has the ingredients to improve a situation. There is still a dispute, but the people involved focus on finding a solution that benefits everyone. These are known as "win/win" resolutions.

Constructive conflict is characterized by what the Greek philosopher Aristotle called deliberate discourse. This

approach involves the discussion of advantages and dis-
advantages of a decision. It features a willingness to blend
ideas. Constructive conflict is also marked by honest communication and mutual respect. "One of the most important
skills [in managing conflict] is to be able to disagree with
each other's ideas while confirming one another's personal
competence," explains Dean Tjosvold, a professor of management and a conflict resolution scholar.

The Nature Conservancy, for example, often uses constructive conflict in its efforts to protect the environment. This
environmental organization works to preserve natural areas
around the world. Often, environmental issues pit environmentalists against companies. Companies might complain
that environmental groups are uncaring about the economic
needs of people, communities, and businesses. On the other
side, environmental groups are highly critical of companies
that harm endangered wildlife and ecosystems.

The conservancy takes a constructive approach to these
conflicts. The organization partners with people and businesses to develop creative ways to protect the environment.
Companies may fund the conservancy's scientific research,
for example, and might also purchase land that is then protected and managed by the conservancy.

In one example from 1992, the conservancy teamed up
with the drug company Pfizer. The company had a bad reputation for polluting air and water around Groton, Connecti-
cut. Environmental groups had criticized the company for
the environmental damage it had caused. Pfizer decided to
launch a multimillion-dollar project to reduce pollution. As
part of that effort, it gave a $60,000 grant to the conservancy
to research ways to best protect the marshlands there.

When the deal was announced, the executive director of
the Nature Conservancy, Leslie N. Corey, said, "We need to
strike a balance between the needs of people and society,
and the needs of the environment. If we are going to preserve nature, we have to find a way for humans to pursue

our needs." Through this constructive conflict, the Nature Conservancy and Pfizer fashioned a solution that benefited both sides. By working with the conservancy, Pfizer found an ally to help it reduce pollution. The partnership also softened criticism that the company did not care about the environment. For its part, the conservancy had created a new ally in its efforts to conserve the wetlands around Groton. Both sides in this constructive conflict came out ahead.

SELECTIVE PERCEPTION AND CONFLICT

Judging conflict can be a thorny business. Individuals' own beliefs and relationships can strongly color their opinions about an experience. A 1950s experiment about a football game explored this natural human trait.

In 1951, the Dartmouth Indians and Princeton Tigers played a hard-fought college football game marked by heavy penalties and injuries on both sides. Afterward, a pair of psychologists studied the impressions of the game held by students from Princeton and Dartmouth. The groups, having watched the same game, had very different interpretations of the action. Princeton students were more likely to think that the Dartmouth players had played too roughly. Most Dartmouth students came to the opposite conclusion; they blamed the Princeton players.

The researchers concluded that, psychologically, people tend to take the side of the group to which they are related or connected. In other words, personal history and relationships can affect how people understand what they see, hear, and experience. People are much more likely to agree with and support "their side" in a conflict. In psychology, this phenomenon is known as selective perception. Selective perception can have a major effect on a conflict. Finding a constructive resolution will prove very difficult if the two sides are unwilling to consider other opinions or concerns. This phenomenon highlights the need to understand the other side's viewpoints.

Disputes do not always divide cleanly into destructive or constructive categories. At times they may shift from one to the other. Knowledge of what turns conflicts destructive or constructive offers people the chance to seek the positive path.

THE CUBAN MISSILE CRISIS

The 1962 Cuban Missile Crisis showcases the complex nature of managing conflict. It also clearly demonstrates the need for mature conflict resolution skills among world leaders.

In 1959, Fidel Castro led a communist revolution in Cuba. The incident shocked and embarrassed leaders in the United States, who feared communist expansion in the world. The main communist superpower at the time, the Soviet Union, strongly supported Castro. Then, in 1961, the United States backed a small army of Cuban exiles who were against communism and planned to invade Cuba and overthrow Castro. The attack failed miserably, but it signaled to the Soviets that the United States was willing to use force to try to install a pro-U.S. government in Cuba. Placing missiles in Cuba was part of the Soviets' strategy to block this.

After a U.S. spy plane spotted missile sites in Cuba, President Kennedy alerted the Soviet foreign minister that the United States was aware of the bases. At first the Soviets denied being involved. Then they explained that the missiles were for defending Cuba against U.S. aggression. By October 19, 1962, more U.S. spy plane photos showed that four of the missile sites were finished and ready to be used.

Kennedy and his advisers believed strongly that they could not allow such destructive weapons so close to the U.S. mainland. They plotted three military options: bomb the missile bases, invade Cuba, or prevent ships with military materials from reaching Cuba. All of these options posed grave risks. An attack on Cuba might prompt the Soviets to launch the missiles there, or to strike U.S. forces in Europe. The confrontation had a real possibility of turning into World War III. Military units on all sides were put on high alert.

The Soviets, led by Premier Nikita Khrushchev, had their own dilemmas. If they pulled the missiles out of Cuba, would the United States then invade Cuba? Would the Soviet Union look weak, inviting challenges by others? On the other hand, if Soviet forces did retaliate to a U.S. attack, that meant war— possibly nuclear war. Both sides were tangled in a dangerous predicament.

President Kennedy put a naval quarantine into effect on October 23. Soviet ships did not challenge it. Meanwhile, U.S. and Soviet officials were communicating and carefully negotiating to try to defuse the crisis. So far, though, they had found little upon which to agree.

A shift came on October 26. The Americans received a letter from Khrushchev. In it, he said that the Soviets would remove the missiles from Cuba *if* the United States made a public guarantee that it would not invade Cuba. At the same time, there were reports that the Soviets were speeding up the construction of additional Cuban missile sites. The next day, the Americans received another letter from Khrushchev in which he made an additional condition for a settlement. This demand would remain secret for years. That same day, October 27, other circumstances pushed the conflict to a still more dangerous level. In one incident, a U.S. spy plane was shot down over Cuba and the pilot was killed.

In another, separate mishap, a U-2 spy plane from the United States accidentally flew into Soviet air space near the Arctic Circle. The pilot had been blinded by the Northern Lights and this made it difficult to navigate. Soviet fighter jets scrambled to shoot it down. The U-2 escaped and barely made it back to Alaska. The next day, Khrushchev wrote to Kennedy that the U.S. jet could have been mistaken "for a nuclear bomber, which might push us to a fateful step." Amazingly, this incident would remain secret for more than 45 years.

The near misses seem to have shocked both sides into backing away from the edge. On October 28, the United States guaranteed that it would not invade Cuba. The Soviets promised to remove their missiles from Cuba. A settlement was reached. Both superpowers got something they wanted and escaped embarrassment. The world could breathe a little easier.

The secret part of the deal was that the United States agreed to pull its own nuclear missiles out of Turkey, a country that bordered the Soviet Union. The Americans, though, had asked the Soviets not to reveal that this was part of the agreement. They did not want to appear to have been blackmailed by the Soviets. It was not until 1989 that this tradeoff became public knowledge.

Another result of the Cuban Missile Crisis was a "hotline" between U.S. and Soviet leaders. Though the Soviet Union broke up in 1991, this text-messaging system is still up and running between Russia and the United States. In the words of U.S. Secretary of Defense Robert Gates, it will remain necessary "as long as these two sides have submarines roaming the oceans and missiles pointed at each other." Communication has always been the best means for keeping conflict out of the destructive zone.

UNDERSTANDING 2
CONFLICTS CLOSE
TO HOME

> To put the world right in order, we must first
> put the nation in order; to put the nation in
> order, we must first put the family in order;
> to put the family in order, we must first cul-
> tivate our personal life; we must first set
> our hearts right.
>
> —*Confucius, Chinese philosopher (551–479 B.C.)*

In Part I of the play *Henry IV* by William Shakespeare, the king is very disappointed in his son, Prince Hal. Hal has spent his rebellious youth hanging out with Falstaff, a witty slob, and his crew of scoundrels. While Hal has been party-ing, though, the kingdom has come under threat from rebels. Hal, the eldest son and next in line to the throne, has been replaced by a younger brother in the king's councils. A sad-dened and angry King Henry confronts Hal. He firmly talks to the prince about his crude behavior and how people no longer respect him: "For thou has lost thy princely privilege / With vile participation: not an eye / But is a-weary of thy common sight. . . ." He goes so far as to accuse Hal of being willing to join the rebels against the kingdom.

The confrontation stuns Prince Hal. At first he blames others for turning his father against him. Finally, though, he accepts responsibility. He vows to change and give up his bad habits. In the end, Prince Hal bravely leads the king's forces in defeating the rebel army.

As both Confucius and Shakespeare suggest, there are powerful links between family life and the wider world. Society reflects many of the issues people face in their homes. This can be especially true in matters of conflict and conflict resolution. Disputes all share similar characteristics, whether they are disputes between a parent and child, or between countries. To understand how conflict unfolds on local, national, and global stages, it is helpful to examine how it plays out closer to home.

For most young people, their families are where they first observe and learn life skills. These range from abilities as basic as walking and talking to expressing emotions and developing a value system about how to live. Even tiny babies study, listen, and imitate the people around them. The lessons and habits people learn as small children remain powerful patterns even into adulthood.

Home, of course, is also where most children first experience conflict. Small children naturally bump into limits as they begin exploring the world. One of the first words they learn is *no*, as adults tell them what they should and should not do. A child's desire for a candy bar, for instance, may cross the parents' rules about healthy eating. A teen's wish for a later curfew may run into parental concerns about safety. "Many times, as children mature and want to express more power, conflict increases between parents and children," explains family psychologist Erik A. Fisher. "At this time, primarily when their children are in their early teens, parents often fear that their child may make unwise choices, and they seek to gain more control over their child. As parents seek more control, their children continue to seek more power."

In the home, constructive conflict can bring family members closer together as they work through differences. It can contribute to feelings of trust, security, and connection. Destructive conflict can have the opposite effect. It can trigger feelings of helplessness, sadness, resentment, and anger. It can pull family members apart.

THE EFFECTS OF FAMILY CONFLICT ON CHILDREN

Research has found that children are very sensitive to conflict. Babies of a few months old react when they sense tension around them. They may cry or become more alert when people argue or tempers flare. This is true even if the dispute does not involve the child.

Studies indicate that many children also respond to conflict with increased aggression. If a child is present when adults have an angry confrontation, he or she is more likely to act out by fighting. Psychologist E. Mark Cummings and a team of researchers have examined this effect. In one experiment, two toddlers were playing together peacefully. Then, two actors entered the room and pretended to have an angry argument. When the actors left, the researchers noted that the following took place:

> Billy approaches Susan, who is riding a rocking horse. He pulls her backward off the horse. As she gets up he pushes her and then throws her to the ground. He repeatedly pushes her backside and then her face to the floor, despite her crying and screaming. The mothers then intervene.

Other studies have confirmed these findings. The conclusion is that even background anger—anger not directed at the child—can increase the chances that the child will act aggressively. In a sense, aggression is contagious. A tense or angry atmosphere may set the stage for a fight.

VIOLENT VIDEO GAMES AND AGGRESSION

C ar crashes. Gun battles. Wars against alien invaders. There's no question that the makers of video games have loaded their creations with thrills and kills a second. Unfortunately, a review of 20 years of psychological studies indicates that violent games may increase aggressive behavior in children and teens. That finding is part of a report published by the American Psychological Association (APA), the world's largest association of psychologists.

One investigation studied youth who played violent video games for short periods. After just 10 minutes of play, the children reported a jump in aggressive feelings and actions. Another study focused on the behavior of more than 600 eighth and ninth graders. Teachers reported that the teens who spent the most time playing violent video games were generally more hostile than other youth in the study. They were more likely to get into fights with other students, and more likely to argue with teachers and other authority figures.

In the opinion of researchers Jessica Nicoll and Dr. Kevin M. Kieffer, "future research needs to explore why many children and adolescents prefer to play a violent video game rather than play outside, and why certain personalities are drawn to these types of games."

Age limits and rating systems offer some control of who can buy these games, but the popularity of violent video games seems to know no limits. The video game industry overall is expected to bring in nearly $50 billion a year by 2011.

Conflicts within a family can be especially intense because they usually involve close, long-term relationships between people living under the same roof. Conflicts may arise over problems such as who gets the bathroom next, money squabbles, or more painful circumstances, such as divorce and custody fights. Unmet needs for love, belonging, and respect can turn even small disagreements into big arguments.

Family conflicts take three main forms. The first is conflict between adult couples. No matter how much love a couple may share, expectations and goals will conflict. One partner's wish to buy a new car, for instance, may be at odds with the other's desire to save money for the children's college fund. The second conflict is rivalry between siblings. This conflict involves competition between brothers and/or sisters, often for the affection or attention of a parent or parents. An example might be a brother and sister trying for the best report card as a way to win praise and proof of who is smartest. The third kind of family conflict is between parents and their children. This conflict can easily turn into a power struggle. Safety concerns or the parents' desire for control may compete with their child's growing desire for independence. Such conflicts may occur when a child is any age, from the "terrible twos" to adulthood.

When it comes to dealing with conflict, parents usually are their children's first role models. Children are likely to adopt conflict management strategies that they see their parents use. This is true whether these strategies are constructive or destructive. Family conflict sometimes turns hurtful and destructive when the people involved feel incapable of getting what they want and need in other ways. Their frustration may turn into anger and harmful behavior.

Frequent destructive conflict is hard on the family and on children in particular. Studies indicate that children who grow up in homes with constant conflicts are more likely to develop behavior problems. Disputes that turn emotionally or physically abusive are even more damaging. People who do not cope well with conflict may also suffer from feelings of low self-esteem. If they feel bad about themselves, they may be reluctant to stand up for what they need. They may also feel vulnerable and act prickly when interacting with others. If they feel attacked or disrespected, they may lash out.

Children from abusive homes are more likely to use bullying behaviors toward others. These behaviors may include insults, threats, and physical violence. While abuse may seem normal at home, it causes serious problems at school and in other settings. Children who bully others may be shunned by classmates and may find it difficult to make friends. This can add to feelings of loneliness and low self-esteem.

Other children from abusive families may respond differently. They may learn to be "extra good" as a strategy to avoid conflict. Some may attempt to interrupt an argument by clowning around or misbehaving. Whatever the case, members of abusive families often need professional help. A family history of destructive conflict is very difficult to escape without guidance.

Although angry conflict has obvious drawbacks, constantly avoiding conflict brings its own problems. Passive family members may neglect their own needs rather than strive to get them met. Frustration and resentment may build up and then erupt in angry fights.

Constructive conflict, in contrast, can be healthy for a family. It promotes better understanding, cooperation, and connection among family members. It teaches the children in the family positive and effective ways to stand up for their needs, their opinions, and their beliefs. The keys to constructive conflict within families are good communication and the ability to resolve disputes. Open communication—in which people actively listen and respectfully respond to one another—keeps small problems from becoming big problems. Studies indicate that if disagreements are resolved and harmony is restored, most children will not become upset or aggressive because of conflict in their environment.

Constructive conflict in the home has added advantages as children grow up. It models good conflict resolution skills and gives children a chance to practice them. Mastering these abilities can have a beneficial impact on their futures. It helps build strong friendships, healthy relation-ships at school and work, and, eventually, strong families of their own.

GOOD COMMUNICATION HABITS

Research is clear that good communication improves the chances of keeping a conflict constructive. Here are tips about effective communication with family members.

* Don't bring up difficult issues when people are stressed or in a hurry. If something important needs to be talked about, schedule a time when there won't be interruptions.
* Start conversations by sharing thoughts instead of asking questions.
* Don't interrupt the speaker. Let people finish their point before responding.
* Let people know you're really listening by making eye contact, nodding, and occasionally saying "Okay," or "I hear what you're saying."
* In your own words, repeat back what you heard the other person say. This makes it clearer that you understood his or her point.
* If you don't understand what the other person meant, ask questions to clarify.
* Don't disagree too strongly. People will be less open if they sense anger or defensiveness. Make it clear that it's okay to disagree.
* Talk *with* the other person, not *at* them. Don't lecture, accuse, or insult.
* Monitor your own body language and facial expressions. For example, don't fold your arms or frown while the other person is speaking.
* If you feel like you're going to lose your temper, take a break and ask to meet again later.

CONFLICT MANAGEMENT STYLES

As people grow up, they develop their own ways of dealing with conflict. These conflict management styles are usually products of personality, experience, and family influences. For example, a shy person from a family that avoids conflict may also develop a style that avoids conflict.

Conflict management styles can be divided into five groups. These are:

- ❋ **Submissive:** This style is very passive and cooperative. A submissive person tends to give in to others during conflict. Being submissive often defuses big arguments, but it can also shut down constructive debate. When people are too submissive, they may feel that others take advantage of them. This can lead to anger and resentfulness.
- ❋ **Evasive:** People with this style are likely to withdraw from most confrontations. They may come across as calm or relaxed, but they are often passive and avoid conflict—even constructive conflicts that could benefit their lives. Like submissive types, they may build up anger and resentfulness.
- ❋ **Collaborative:** A collaborative style is assertive. It blends strong, clear opinions with an enjoyment of teamwork. A person with this style asks lots of questions and seeks new information to get a clear picture of the situation. He or she demonstrates creativity and respect for others when solving a problem. One potential weakness: This person can get bogged down in the conflict resolution process instead of getting the conflict resolved.
- ❋ **Competitive:** People with this style are very aggressive and clear about what they want. Generally, combative people do not care very much about the opinions of others. As a result, they may get things done, but their competitiveness can

discourage agreement and cooperation. This can lead to more conflict with others. It can also drive away friends and colleagues.

❄ **Cooperative:** A cooperative style may be either passive or assertive. A person with this style usually comes across as very reasonable. He or she is likely to search for a middle position that will meet most people's needs in a conflict. At the same time, giving in too easily can limit creativity when solving a problem. Being too cooperative may ignore bigger troubles and leave the cooperative person's own needs unmet.

Each style has its own strengths and weaknesses. A person may use different styles to deal with different situations. When dealing with conflict, it is often helpful to identify the conflict management styles of the people involved. This can improve the chances of reaching a resolution that meets the needs of the different sides.

TEACHING CONFLICT RESOLUTION SKILLS TO YOUNG CHILDREN

Good conflict resolution skills are very beneficial to families. Unfortunately, these skills are rarely taught directly. Says Erik A. Fisher, a family psychologist: "We go to school to learn how to read and write; we go to church to learn about God and morality; we go to college to study topics related to our possible career interests; but no one teaches us how to live in a family."

Some programs are striving to change this. One example is the Peaceful Kids Early Childhood Social-Emotional Learning (ECSEL) curriculum. ECSEL teaches relationship skills to preschool children, their parents, and their teachers. The program helps "the child understand both [his or] her own and the other person's feelings and perspective, as well as the consequences of [his or] her action, rather than simply getting the child to obey." ECSEL introduces preschoolers to words and ideas about feelings, cooperation, and problem solving.

The program teaches these things through a variety of activities. Children perform cooperative projects that require teamwork. Another goal of the program is to help young children recognize and act on ideas about right and wrong. Problem solving often involves some conflict resolution. To teach this, ECSEL uses what it calls the STAR model: "*stop* and think, *tell* how you feel, *ask* what we can do, and *resolve* the situation." Instead of reacting impulsively, children are taught to think and use their feelings to decide the right thing to do.

Parents and teachers are taught to clearly explain rules and consequences. The adults also practice more effective ways of disciplining children. They learn to correct children as an expression of cooperation and affection, not of impatience and disappointment.

The overall idea of ECSEL is to create a team—children, parents, and teachers—that works together to help everyone succeed. Again, effective communication is the key. That is why teaching the preschoolers how to express their thoughts and feelings is an important part of the curriculum.

Studies of the program have shown that it helps improve communication and cooperation between children and their parents and teachers, and among the children themselves. ECSEL's creators, Sandra V. Sandy and Kathleen M. Cochran, think that teaching these skills to children when they are preschoolers is better than waiting until they are older. It gives children the tools to develop better relationships as they grow up.

Learning techniques for handling conflicts benefits all family members. If adults have good conflict management skills, they will feel more confident and calm when parenting. They can then teach and model these valuable skills for their children. This is excellent preparation for bigger challenges as young people move beyond the family circle.

MANAGING CONFLICTS IN FRIENDSHIPS

3

> When we hurt each other, we should write it down in the sand, so the winds of forgiveness can make it go away for good. When we help each other we should chisel it in stone, lest we never forget the love of a friend.
>
> —Christian H. Godefroy, French author

In the 2003 animated movie *Finding Nemo*, a stressed-out fish named Marlin sets out across the ocean to find his lost son, Nemo. Along the way, Marlin always expects the worst and does not trust kindness or friendship. He frequently shouts at Dory, the sweet but scatterbrained surgeonfish that tags along on his quest. The pair does a lousy job of managing interpersonal conflict, made worse by Dory's terrible memory. She can't remember half of the nitpicky things Marlin says to her.

Dory and Marlin rescue each other several times. A host of friendly creatures also aid them on their journey. By the end of the movie, Marlin has found Nemo and learned an important lesson. He recognizes the strength and comfort that comes with friendship. Because of his new experiences, he becomes a better friend and father.

Marlin, already a dad, is a little old to be finally recognizing the value of friendship. Friends are usually a young child's first relationships outside his or her family circle. For teens, making good friends is a big step in building independence on the way toward adulthood.

Research has proven the power and importance of friendship. Friendship helps people develop in many ways. Friends support each other as they learn to cope with stress and emotions. They help one another solve problems. Friendships allow young people to refine social skills that they will rely on throughout their lives. Besides being a source of laughter and comfort, friendship helps people grow into healthy, happy grown-ups. In fact, studies indicate that the ability of a child to make friends is the best guarantee that she or he will be a happy adult.

What does all of that have to do with managing conflicts? When it comes to building friendships, conflict resolution skills are essential. This is especially true during the teen years, when developing skills to resolve conflicts is the key to teens' social development. Teens who can communicate well and resolve conflicts are more likely to develop friendships.

Conflict with friends and peers can be a source of learning and growth. "Truth springs from argument amongst friends," the Scottish philosopher David Hume once said. Friendships can be great arenas for playful challenges to ideas, thoughts, and behaviors. Friends help each other discover new points of view and explore new interests. Constructive conflict resolution requires trust, and trust and loyalty are characteristics of strong friendships.

When people lack confidence in their ability to cope with conflict, though, they are less open to new experiences. They may shy away from meeting and learning from people with different interests and backgrounds. This may interfere with making friends and can get in the way of clear communication. That, oddly enough, can lead to misunderstanding and conflict.

Peer pressure is a common source of conflict among friends. Peer pressure is not always bad, though. Friends can push one another to study harder or try new activities such as sports, music, and drama. Good friends also confront one another about bad or harmful habits. They may express concern to a friend if he or she has started smoking, drinking, abusing drugs, or being mean to others.

Dealing with negative peer pressure poses a greater challenge. The desire to fit in and belong is strong in most people. "Group-think" can stop a person from disagreeing with or walking away from a situation that he or she finds disturbing. People might not want to be labeled as outsiders or afraid. Such fear of being labeled can sway them to do things that go against their feelings, beliefs, and values. Conflict resolution skills provide tools to counter negative peer pressure. That is one of many reasons educators and child development professionals are encouraging more and better instruction about conflict resolution.

RESOLVING CONFLICTS WITH FRIENDS

It happens often on the playground: Two young children get into a squabble. Right away, an adult steps in to deal with it. The older a child gets, though, the more he or she needs to resolve conflicts without another person's help. There won't always be an "authority figure" around to enforce a resolution. Young people need to learn how to manage their own conflicts.

Studies show a big overlap between good friendship skills and good conflict resolution skills. These include:

* The ability to recognize and respond to the emotions of a peer
* A willingness to cooperate

* The ability to actively listen and respond appropriately
* The ability to express ideas

Some young people seem to come by these abilities naturally, but research also shows that conflict resolution skills can be taught and learned. Like all talents and abilities, these skills improve with experience and practice.

Disputes with friends naturally trigger anxiety and dread. The fear of losing a close friendship is powerful and can make friends reluctant to address a problem. What psychologists have found, however, is that tackling and resolving a conflict often leads to a stronger bond between friends. It proves that the friendship is not just the fair-weather sort, but one that can survive tough times, too.

Psychologists and sociologists have been studying interpersonal conflict for decades. The general agreement is that constructive conflict resolution between people works best if it respects a few simple guidelines. These include:

* **Cooling off:** In a conflict between friends, the two should not try to resolve the dispute while tempers are still hot.
* **Identifying the root of the conflict:** Before sitting down to talk, friends should be honest with themselves about the source of the conflict. Is it about something that the other person did or didn't do? Or does it have more to do with a sense of disappointment about something that happened? A personal disappointment can often lead an individual to blame others.
* **Dealing with the conflict:** The friends should set up a time to talk in private. Both should present their feelings and views without blaming or accusing.

❁ **Getting the facts and feelings:** When the two friends meet, they should carefully listen to what the other says—no interruptions allowed. The most important thing is to gather information without judging.

❁ **Work together to create a resolution:** Together, the two friends should focus on creating a resolution that benefits them both in the best way possible. Brainstorming ideas can help them come up with options. Ideally, friends in a conflict should think of themselves as a team working together to solve a problem.

The process above might sound complicated, but it creates a useful outline for keeping the conversation focused. Also, the more often conflict resolution skills are practiced, the easier and more effective they become.

Imagine these conflict resolution skills at work between two friends:

Anna: Thanks for studying with me. This is really helping me get ready for the test.

Al: Yeah, well, it isn't doing me much good. I'm not learning anything from you.

Anna: Wow.

Al: What?

Anna: We have to talk. I feel hurt when you say that I'm not smart.

Al: Can't you understand that I'm just really stressed out about this test? I have to get an A!

Anna: Wait, let me finish. I'd be upset, too, but the way you roll your eyes and make fun of me is really hurtful. I know I'm not great at studying, but I'm trying as hard as I can.

Al: I know. I guess what you are saying is that you feel like I don't respect your feelings. I'm sorry, but I'm really stressed out.

Anna: I can understand that. Let's work together so we are both calm and do well on the test.

Al: Okay, how about this: I'll try to be more considerate and not put you down.

Anna: Okay. Also, a compliment every once in a while would go a long way.

Al: Okay. Actually, studying with you is helping me, too, because I find new ways to consider things as I explain them to you.

Anna: Great! And, listen, I'll try to take better notes so I don't forget so much and ask so many questions. Fair?

Al: Sounds good!

CONFLICT BETWEEN COUPLES

Tony and Emily have been going out for a few weeks, and he is beginning to act like he owns her. He complains when she spends time with her best friend—or anyone except him. He expects her to meet him in the hallways between classes, eat lunch with him, let him go home with her after school, and be with him every weekend. Afraid she'll lose him, Emily begins to cut herself off from her friends.

That scenario is taken from *Love Doesn't Have to Hurt,* a publication by the American Psychological Association. This booklet describes situations related to dating and conflict. It also outlines ways for teens to protect themselves if a relationship turns abusive or violent.

As children grow into teenagers and then adults, dating is often a natural outgrowth of friendship. Going out with someone and becoming more than just friends can be thrilling experiences. New feelings of affection and love bring fresh energy to life. "No, there's nothing half so sweet in life as love's young dream," wrote the Irish poet Thomas Moore.

MARTIAL ARTS FOR PEACE

Video games and films can make the martial arts look anything but peaceful. They often portray incredible violence.

Studies indicate, however, that people who actually practice martial arts in real life feel less aggressive and more self-confident. Part of the reason seems to come with learning more than punches, kicks, and blocks. Most schools of martial arts—including karate, judo, tae kwon do, jujitsu, and others—also teach respect, self-awareness, and self-control. Research credits martial arts teachers with having a positive effect on students. The instructors model respectful and disciplined behavior toward others and themselves.

Dr. T. Webster Doyle formed Martial Arts for Peace to emphasize these benefits. His organization stresses the positive impact this training can have, especially for young people. His program concentrates on managing conflict resolution, not on fighting.

"Dr. T." describes what he calls the "3Ps" of self-defense:

* **Prevent** a fight from happening by avoiding it.
* **Prepare** to use your brain instead of your fists to resolve it.
* **Protect** yourself by learning how to fight so you don't have to.

Dr. T. believes reducing conflict in the world starts with a commitment from individual people. He sees the martial arts as one of the paths to that more peaceful world. He writes:

Putting aside the tournaments and the sport aspect of the martial arts, . . . can we see that these arts were primarily developed to educate and protect ourselves and our children from harm, to find peaceful ways to relate to each other? And can we see that learning these arts in this manner can help us cope not only with the schoolyard bully but also with the bullying that occurs domestically, socially, and internationally?

Helping people share this vision is the goal of Martial Arts for Peace.

Dating, though, often brings its own unique conflicts. Young people especially may have the expectation that two people in love should not have disagreements. Yet, big and small conflicts occur in every dating relationship. They can

CYBERBULLYING

In the last generation, the Internet has changed everything from dating to music to gossip to how to research school reports. It has revolutionized how information flows between people. Unfortunately, that includes a new brand of bullying.

Cyberbullying uses e-mails, digital pictures, text messages, and other kinds of electronic media to tease and harass victims. Consider these examples: A teen boy has a camera phone picture snapped of him while he gets dressed in a gym changing room. Within minutes, the picture is seen on other people's camera phones around the school. A middle-school student receives a text message teasing her about her clothes. "Where did your mommy buy those shoes—the bargain basement?" the text taunts.

Cyberbullies' main weapons are insults and rumors. Because they can remain anonymous, they often act more viciously than they would if they were face-to-face with their victim. "Cyberbullying follows you everywhere," Parry Aftab told *The Sydney Morning Herald*. Aftab is a legal expert on Internet issues and the founder of WiredSafety.org, an organization that educates people about online safety. "It will follow you home and to [your] grandma's. You can't avoid it by leaving the schoolyard and you never know if it's your best friend or your worst enemy. . . ."

New laws are being put in place to go after cyberbullies. Social networking Web sites, such as Facebook and MySpace, are also making efforts to combat online harassment. They promise to sever links to groups connected to cyberbullying. They also plan to investigate and expel users who harass others. Internet safety experts recommend that people with personal Web pages not reveal any personal information (such as addresses or phone numbers) and not post any information or photos that could be used by a bully.

be as minor as a disagreement about which movie to see, and they can be as major as an argument about sex or drugs. When differences do arise, there is frequently a crisis. Strong feelings often lead to strong reactions.

How can people deal with this kind of abuse once they become a target? If cyberbullying does start, experts advise that people not "return fire" with their own online trash talk. As a rule, bullies of all stripes feed on victims' fear, pain, and fury. That is why targets of bullying should meet the taunts with silence. At the same time they should alert parents, school officials, and the managers of the particular Web site about the abuse.

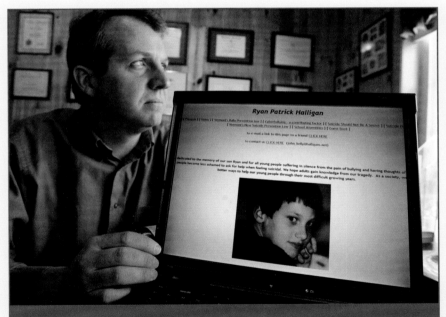

John Halligan displays a Web page dedicated to his 13-year-old son, Ryan. Halligan is certain that cyberbullying played a part in his son's suicide in 2003, after online bullies spread rumors through instant messages. Halligan now works to curb similar behavior.

For ordinary conflict with a boyfriend or girlfriend, the process and skills described earlier may be enough to resolve the conflict: Be calm, discuss feelings and facts, and work together to create a resolution.

In some unfortunate situations, though, dating can become abusive or violent. One study, done in 2000, surveyed 600 students between the ages of 13 and 18. About 37 percent of the boys and 36 percent of the girls reported that they had experienced some physical violence in a dating relationship.

When dating turns abusive, the conflict has gone too far. Action needs to be taken to end the relationship. If necessary, outside help needs to be brought in to guarantee the safety of the victim. The abuser usually needs help to change his or her ways. Abuse is a form of bullying. As a rule, bullies do not stop their abuse unless confronted.

MANAGING CONFLICTS AT SCHOOL

4

Cooperate with each other. Compete only against yourself.

—Harry K. Wong, teacher, author, and publisher

Kaneésha Sonée Johnson did not like what she was seeing. Other black children at her school in Hawthorne, California, were hassling Asian immigrant students. Life might have been easier for this fifth grader if she had ignored the conflict, but Kaneésha decided to take a stand. She showed newcomers how to get along in their new culture. She helped students who didn't know English well do their homework. She told children who picked on her new friends to stop. In time, she even convinced Asian and black students to team up for sports and work together in the classroom.

Kaneésha learned that doing the right thing is not always the easy thing. Some classmates gave her a hard time for her stance. She put on a brave face at school, but sometimes she couldn't help crying when she got home. "I just decided to [get involved] because I know how it feels when people laugh at you," Kaneésha explained. "That old poem says, 'Sticks and stones may break my bones but names can never hurt me,' but some words do hurt."

In 2001, Kaneésha's courage and peacemaking skills caught the attention of the Giraffe Heroes Project. The organization honored her for "sticking her neck out" to help make the world a better place. Not only did she show personal guts and character, but she also helped bring greater understanding and harmony to her school.

Traditionally, schools and classrooms are supposed to focus on academic learning. Students study English, science, art, math, and other subjects. As they near adulthood, they might add subjects to prepare them for specific jobs or careers. As Kaneésha found out, though, school offers other lessons. "Schools are part of, and offer a superb preparation for, 'real life,'" explains British educator Mervyn Flecknoe. "[T]hey can prepare children to become managers of conflict; or alternatively to take the role of either crusher or crushed." It is important for all students to learn how to become a "manager of conflict." Learning how to manage conflicts benefits both students and their school community.

BULLYING IN SCHOOLS

Shockingly violent attacks at schools flood the media from time to time. Shootings at Colorado's Columbine High School in 1999 put a white-hot spotlight on school violence. In that case, a pair of students murdered 12 classmates and a teacher, and wounded dozens of others. In 2005, a 16-year-old student shot and killed seven people at Red Lakes High School in Minnesota.

The extreme violence of events like these has left many people in the United States with the idea that schools are dangerous places. Intense press coverage reinforces that belief. The reality, fortunately, is less frightening, though more complicated. In truth, schools have always been one of the safest places for children and teens to be. "National statistics continue to show that children face greater safety risks outside of school than they do in school," psychologist Marisa Reddy told the U.S. Senate in 2001.

Most in-school disputes are minor. Interactions with classmates and teachers can lead to bruised feelings and irritation. Yet, most of these quarrels can be resolved with an apology, a friendly reconnection, or sometimes by avoidance. Basic conflict resolution skills can keep a small misunderstanding from flaring into an angry argument or worse.

Students (*from left*) Kiera Clarke, Björn Begelman, Emily Doubt, and Reid Erickson sit in a discussion group during their Contemporary Problems class at Nathan Hale High School in Seattle in 2002. They previously discussed a proposed law to make school districts adopt or amend policies to stop harassment in schools. Emily feared that it could be used to prevent classroom discussion of issues such as race, religion, and sexual orientation. Students also felt the bill would not do much to stop bullying in schools.

Bullying takes conflict to a more destructive level, and this weighs heavily on the minds of many students. Bullying at school is the number one fear for 25 percent of students, according to a 2004 *Family Circle* survey. Research has helped reveal the extent of the problem. One government study surveyed students in grades 6 through 10. It showed that approximately 3.2 million young people in the United States were victims of bullying, and approximately 3.7 million had acted as bullies to someone else. These numbers included 1.2 million students who were both victims and bullies. From this information, the researchers conducting the study determined that 30 percent of U.S. students were bullies, victims, or both. Relatedly, a National Crime Prevention Council report notes that 60 percent of U.S. teens witness bullying at school at least once a day. Another study concluded that 160,000 children and teens nationwide stay home from school each day to avoid harassment.

What qualifies as bullying behavior? According to Dan Olweus, a Norwegian social researcher who has studied bullying for many years, bullying has three main characteristics: It involves intentionally picking on others, it is done repeatedly over a period of time, and it targets someone considered weaker. In its report, *Bullying Prevention is Crime Prevention,* the organization Fight Crime: Invest in Kids describes different forms of bullying: "Bullying behavior can be verbal, such as insulting someone or making threats; psychological, such as spreading rumors or shunning the individual; or physical, such as knocking down or hitting the person." Whatever form bullying takes, it can make victims' lives miserable. It also contributes to a climate of conflict in a school.

A bully's actions are meant to intimidate and even terrorize their victims. As a result, a bully's target is likely to suffer from low self-esteem, depression, and a sense of helplessness. Some victims experience suicidal thoughts. "Acts of bullying have profound psychological effects on children," write Sandra Harris and Conley Hathorn in the *National*

Senior Caleb Wilson, a member of Old Forge High School's Peer Mediation Team, asks seventh grader Tyler Clark to sign a pillow for an anti-bullying pledge in 2008. The Pennsylvania high school was one of more than 220 U.S. schools to participate in the first International Stand Up to Bullying Day, in February 2008.

Association of Secondary School Principals Bulletin. They argue that growing up is tough enough before bullying is added to the mix. Along with educational and family responsibilities, children and teens should be exploring their independence as well as new interests. Bullying makes this process much more difficult, say Harris and Hathorn. It often stunts the personal development of victims and it blocks them from experiencing trusting, fun relationships with teachers and peers.

In almost every case, people who bully are haunted by fears and troubles of their own. They also generally suffer from low self-esteem. Research shows that their social skills and academic abilities are often below average. That is small comfort to a bully's victim, of course, and it does not excuse a bully's behavior. At the same time, understanding a bully's motivations can point to ways to help her or him stop the destructive behavior. As the poet Henry Wadsworth Longfellow said, "If we could read the secret history of our enemies, we should find in each life sorrow and suffering enough to disarm all hostility."

A conflict involving bullying can cause a chain reaction of conflict and aggression. A victim may turn around and bully someone weaker or lash out with violence. A U.S. Secret Service investigation concluded that almost 75 percent of school shootings have been carried out by attackers who felt "persecuted, bullied, threatened, attacked, or injured by others prior to the incident." Reducing bullying is an issue of school safety and public safety.

After the 1999 Columbine High School attack, many political leaders were so shocked that they took action. They passed new laws in hopes of stopping violence and bullying in schools. Urged on by panicked parents, many schools established "zero-tolerance" policies. These rules suspended or expelled students for any violent behavior or threat of violence.

Since then, zero-tolerance policies have received heavy criticism. Critics and even some supporters have complained that the rules were an overreaction to the threat. These policies often require automatic, harsh punishment. Many school districts eliminated the creative problem solving that is a main characteristic of good conflict resolution. In one case, a 10-year-old Colorado girl reported herself when she accidentally brought a small knife to school in her lunch box. She was automatically expelled. The school district received strong criticism from around the country and eventually reversed its decision.

Zero-tolerance rules also have consequences that were not planned. Students caught acting violently have been thrown out of school and, instead of getting help for stopping their bullying behavior, they have carried their problems into the community. Youth who are considered bullies are much more likely to kill themselves or commit crimes than other teens. One study found that 60 percent of male bullies surveyed had been convicted of at least one crime by age 24.

Supporters had hoped that zero-tolerance policies would prevent bullying and school violence. Critics, however, say that the rules do not prevent conflict—they just catch and punish the bully after he or she has already hurt someone else. Educators and school psychologists have begun supporting creative approaches that focus on preventing violence rather than just reacting to it. Some antiviolence programs seek to reduce in-school disputes by training students in conflict resolution skills. Others include conflict resolution in classroom lessons or school-wide programs. The goal is the same: Make schools a safe place where *all* students want to come and learn.

What should be done about bullying and other in-school conflicts? The answer is not simple, and one solution will not fix every situation. Research has made one point clear, however: Learning conflict resolution skills helps reduce destructive conflict in schools. "There is now much evidence from school systems of the positive effects of conflict resolution training on the students who were trained," writes Morton Deutsch in *The Handbook of Conflict Resolution*. Deutsch is one of the world's top scholars on the subject. He founded the International Center for Cooperation and Conflict Resolution at Columbia University in New York City.

Conflict resolution programs in schools take two main forms. The first and most common is peer mediation. This approach trains a team of peer mediators in conflict resolution skills. These teams then apply their skills to help fellow students settle their disputes. The other popular approach is called a whole-school program. This kind of program involves efforts to build the members of the school body (students, teachers, staff, and parents) into cooperative, supportive communities.

MYTHS AND FACTS ABOUT BULLYING

Conflicts that involve bullying are some of the most painful and difficult disputes to resolve. They usually require outside intervention to stop the abuse. Here are several myths and facts about bullying explained at www.bullying.org, a site created by Canadian teacher Bill Belsey as a response to school violence.

Myth: "Bullying is just a stage, a normal part of life. . . ."
Fact: Bullying is not "normal" or socially acceptable behavior. We give bullies power by accepting this behavior.

Myth: "If I tell someone, it will just make it worse."
Fact: Research shows that bullying will stop when adults in authority and peers get involved.

Myth: "Just stand up for yourself and hit them back."
Fact: There are some times when people can be forced to defend themselves, but hitting back usually makes the bullying worse and increases the risk for serious physical harm.

Myth: "Bullying is a school problem. The teachers should handle it."
Fact: Bullying is a broader social problem that often happens outside of schools: on the street, at shopping centers, the local pool, summer camp, and even in the adult workplace.

Myth: "People are born bullies."
Fact: Bullying is a learned behavior, and behaviors can be changed.

PEER MEDIATION

According to the National Association for Mediation in Education (NAME), the purpose and value of peer mediation is "to teach students how to deal with anger constructively, how to communicate feelings and concerns without using violence and abusive language, how to think critically about alternative solutions, and how to agree to solutions in which all parties win."

In 2004, Sacred Heart School in Bellevue, Washington, introduced peer mediation to its students and faculty. Principal Carola Wittmann had noticed an unsettled feeling when she first took her job at Sacred Heart. "I noted a student body that was very bright and also had a lot of conflicts," she told a reporter from *The Catholic Northwest Progress*. "And I saw a lot of [students] not being open to another person's tendencies or shortcomings or strengths."

Sacred Heart brought in trainers from the Conflict Resolution Unlimited (CRU) Institute. This organization trains adults and young people in conflict mediation skills. In Sacred Heart's case, CRU trained 24 seventh and eighth graders as peer mediators. Chosen for their good listening skills, these teens were trained to work in pairs. They would listen as the students involved in a conflict shared their perceptions of their argument. The mediators would help members of each side express what they were thinking and feeling. Mediators would also referee to keep the interaction polite and fair. If possible, the teen mediators would then guide the two sides toward a resolution upon which both could agree.

One of the strengths of peer mediation is how it uses student insights to solve student conflict. "When you're with a teacher or principal, you get intimidated and kind of hold back your thoughts," said Sacred Heart eighth grader and peer mediator Nick Aigner. "[But] when you're with other students you can express your feelings a little [better]." A long-term benefit of peer mediation is the lifelong skills it teaches students. According to educator Mervyn Flecknoe, many of the skills needed for peer mediation are the same skills that help students get good jobs later on in life when they finish school. These skills include critical thinking, problem solving, and learning how to get along with a variety of people.

Peer mediation programs do have their weaknesses. One weakness seems to be the kind of students selected to be mediators, program experts have said. Often only the "best and the brightest students" are selected, according to professors Philip S. Morse and Allen E. Ivey in their book *Face to Face: Communication and Conflict Resolution in the Schools*. Morse and Ivey argue that this may weaken the program because "[C]onflicts are not limited to select students, but occur at each grade level and within each academic and social group. Because students in conflict will be most comfortable relating to others they view as their peers, it is strongly recommended that students be selected from a cross-section of the school community."

WHOLE-SCHOOL CONFLICT RESOLUTION PROGRAMS

Some schools are making the effort to include conflict resolution training in their regular classes. These school-wide programs introduce conflict resolution ideas to all students. There are workshops that include group activities and role-playing to allow students to practice their skills.

Teachers, staff, administrators, and parents may receive separate instruction. Research suggests that teachers themselves often feel unprepared to deal with bullying. Since bullies rarely harass schoolmates in front of adults, teachers may not know how to spot the harm being done. In some cases, the teachers may feel intimidated by a situation, too. In order to confront in-school conflict and feel confident doing so, adults in a school also need training and practice.

The Olweus Bullying Prevention Program provides this kind of instruction. Dan Olweus, a pioneer in studies of bullying and school conflicts, designed the program. It has proven to work in Europe and the United States, but it is not a quick fix. The recommended timeline for introducing this program stretches over two years.

The Olweus program addresses in-school conflict at every level: school-wide, in the classroom, and between individuals. The goal of this and other such programs is to turn the whole school into a team of students, teachers, staff, and

MICHAEL HWU AND SAVE

In 1993, two police cars and an ambulance with flashing lights were in front of Michael Hwu's house one day when he came home from school. Three teens had robbed his family's home in Pasadena, California. They had also beaten his father and shot him in the leg. Michael's father recovered, but the sight of his dad in a hospital bed—his face swollen and his leg in a cast—burned itself into the memory of the 15-year-old.

A short time later, Michael's family moved to Seattle, Washington. They sought a fresh start, but Michael could not forget what had happened. "I knew I couldn't just sit on the sidelines anymore," he said in the book *What Do You Stand For?* "I had to do something about violence."

He contacted Students Against Violence Everywhere (SAVE). This youth-led organization encourages student activism to promote peace and conflict management. Michael wrote a proposal for starting a chapter of SAVE at his high school. His principal approved the new organization. Through SAVE, Michael then organized a series of school forums on violence and youth.

Michael also vowed to himself not to look the other way when conflict flared. In one incident at a school dance, he witnessed a friend and another youth get into a shouting and pushing match. Michael immediately stepped in and told them to stop. "That was all it took," he said later. "They just need someone to step in so no one looked bad in front of their friends."

parents who care about and look after each other. All members of this team should feel inspired to stop aggressive, abusive behavior.

Susan Limber helped introduce the Olweus program in the United States. She describes the program's approach: "To reduce bullying at a school, requires a culture change at the school…. I think the most effective programs are those that are very comprehensive, that involve not just the students and a classroom teacher but every adult at a school. The bus drivers should feel they have a role in bullying prevention, a cafeteria worker, certainly the parents should feel they have a role in helping to create a bully-free atmosphere at the school."

Not all schools are introducing these changes. There are many reasons why some schools don't, and some of them are complex. Such programs are costly and time-consuming. Many schools run short of money and class time. Decision-makers may argue that this time would be better spent studying and preparing for tests.

Both peer mediation and whole-school conflict resolution programs also call for a big commitment on the part of school administrators. School officials must give students and teachers more say and power in how a school is run. Some officials may disapprove of such changes and resist them.

Convincing people to change how they view and manage conflict can be a difficult task. People often prefer to stick with the way things are. Introducing major changes in a school requires equal parts leadership, diplomacy, courage, and determination.

MANAGING CONFLICTS IN COMMUNITIES

5

When spider webs unite, they can halt even a lion.

—*African proverb*

Traditionally, the San people have roamed across the arid regions of southern Africa. These hunter-gatherers, sometimes called Bushmen, live in bands of about 25 people. When the San people recognize tension in their group, they intervene quickly. Family members encourage those involved in a conflict to talk to each other. Elders are called on to offer their experience and advice.

If the dispute cannot be worked out in direct talks, elders may call for a *xotla*. This is a public meeting to discuss the conflict. It acts as a form of mediation. The people involved have a chance to air their feelings and complaints in front of friends and family. All adults can share their views and thoughts.

A xotla may last for several days. The goal is not to judge who is right and who is wrong. It does not seek to shame or punish anyone. Its goal is to reach "a solution that meets the needs of everyone and that everyone can support," says

William L. Ury, a conflict resolution researcher who has studied the San. More often than not, the xotla resolves the conflict. The people in the dispute share public apologies and forgiveness. In this way, the San people heal divisions in their community.

COMMUNITY CONFLICTS

Communities form wherever people or groups interact in public life. Humans are social creatures who naturally create relationships and alliances. At different times, people or groups will work shoulder to shoulder for a common goal. At other times, groups will oppose each other, causing conflict.

Community disputes are usually more complex than interpersonal conflicts. Most people belong to multiple communi-

NOT IN OUR TOWN

Billings, Montana, is a city of a little fewer than 100,000 people. It has a reputation for small-town friendliness. In the early 1990s, though, Billings experienced a spike in hate crimes. White racists began to distribute leaflets with hateful messages and threats. They vandalized the local Jewish cemetery. They painted "Die, Indian, Die" on the house of a Native American family. A group of racist skinheads entered a church with a mostly black congregation during services and stood silently in the back as a way to intimidate churchgoers.

Sheriff Wayne Inman and others in the community knew they had to take a stand. Hundreds of volunteers showed up to paint over hate-speech graffiti. White supporters attended the black church to counter the threat. "[H]ate groups have learned from experience that if a community doesn't respond, then the community accepts [what they're doing]," Sheriff Inman said. "Silence is acceptance to them."

The community began to organize. People planned anti-hate rallies. Hundreds marched behind a banner that read, "STAND TOGETHER BILLINGS!" Yet, the racists' hateful actions continued. On December 2,

ties. They might belong to a school community and also a religious community, for example. These communities may exist within a neighborhood. The neighborhood sits within a larger community, perhaps a town, suburb, or city. The town, suburb, or city sits within a county, and that sits within a state or province, and so on.

Community disputes sometimes center on cultural or ethnic differences. An example of this is when people in a community are upset and annoyed that new arrivals do not speak the local language. Other community conflicts may revolve around how land is used. Still others may deal with jobs, pollution, taxes, services such as public transportation, and noise that disturbs the neighbors.

Community disputes usually begin with hidden tension. An example might be a neighbor who is annoyed with the

1993, a chunk of cinder block shattered the bedroom window of a five-year-old Jewish boy. In his window was a picture of a menorah, the nine-candled symbol of the Jewish holiday of Hanukkah.

To show their unity with the Jewish community, some Christian families and churches drew menorahs and taped them into windows. Businesses made photocopies of menorahs and did the same. The idea caught on. Then the *Billings Gazette* printed a full-page image of a menorah in its newspaper. Thousands of homes and businesses hung the picture in their windows. In the face of a united community, the hate crimes dwindled.

Songwriter Fred Small penned the song "Not in Our Town" to spread the message beyond Billings:

One moment of conviction, one voice quiet and clear,
One act of compassion, it all begins here.
No safety now in silence, we've got to stand our ground.
No hate. No violence. Not in our town.

loud music from the house next door. After a while, an event may bring the conflict into the open—perhaps a window-shaking party that wakes up all the other neighbors on a Saturday night.

In general, the conflict can go one of three ways at this point. The best case is that it will lead to constructive resolution. In the aforementioned example, this might consist of a polite but firm phone call from the neighbors to the party house. The loud neighbors would then respond by apologizing and turning down the music.

The conflict could also develop into a power struggle. In this instance, the neighbors may call the loud people next door, but they refuse to turn down the music. So the neighbor calls the police. A squad car pulls up and orders the music turned off. Chances are that both sides will not like this outcome: The neighbors are upset because the people next door refused to turn down the music, while the people next door are upset because they are now in trouble with the police. The conflict is now at a real risk of growing more intense and negative.

Without good conflict resolution skills, the power struggle may escalate and become destructive. Perhaps the neighbors choose to avoid conflict at first by not discussing their concerns in a calm, respectful manner. Instead, they suffer in silence—but their annoyance grows. One day the neighbors and the people next door exchange angry words and insults. Perhaps it turns into a shoving match. The conflict has now spun out of control and turned destructive.

Good conflict resolution management can keep such disputes from turning into a violent confrontation. If the sides cannot reach a solution on their own, many communities offer mediation services that can help.

THE THIRD SIDE

Conflict resolution experts are exploring a new idea of how to deal with disputes. Their idea is called the Third Side. It proposes that other areas of the community have a part in helping people resolve their conflicts.

In U.S. culture, there is a tradition of thinking that conflict only has two sides: good guys versus bad guys, teens versus parents, Republicans versus Democrats, environmentalists versus oil companies. The list goes on. The assumption seems to be that there are only two opinions from which to choose. It also suggests that one side is right and the other is wrong. This idea of conflict is often supported by news coverage, movies, books, sports, video games, and other forms of popular culture.

What if there was another side—a third side that could guide or prod the other two toward more constructive inter-action? This is a question posed by William L. Ury, the direc-tor of the Global Negotiation Project at Harvard Law School. He is a leading scholar in the field of conflict and conflict resolution. There is a third side to almost every conflict, Ury explains. This side consists of people who are affected by the conflict, but who may not be directly involved. In schools, the third side might include peer mediators. In that noisy dispute between neighbors discussed earlier, it might be other people living in the neighborhood. In a war between two countries, it might be a neighboring country or an outside ally.

Ury compares the Third Side to the immune system, the body's cells and organs that defend against disease and ill-ness. Instead of controlling diseased cells, though, Third Siders manage conflicts. If possible, they bring them under control and to a constructive resolution. "The Third Side offers a promising new way to look at the conflicts around us," writes Ury. "The Third Side is the community—us—in action protecting our most precious interests in safety and well-being. It suggests . . . practical roles any of us can play on a daily basis to stop destructive fighting. . . . Each of our individual actions is like a single spider web, fragile perhaps but, when united with others, capable of halting the lion of war."

Sarah Swagart took on the role of Third Sider in a dispute in Oak Harbor, Washington. The conflict was between skateboarders and the city. Swagart, then in eighth grade, felt that skaters in Oak Harbor were being treated too harshly. She understood that kickflips and rail grinding along sidewalks and in parking lots could be annoying, but she could not understand why the city treated skaters like criminals. The fines of up to $500 and threats of 90 days in jail seemed too harsh to her.

Sarah was not a skater herself, but she took on the cause. She formed an organization called Nobody Special. The name, she felt, described the skaters as just the average kids they were. The mission of this organization was to get Oak Harbor to build a skate park. She also wanted to help skaters upgrade their public image from punks to skilled athletes.

Sarah disliked public speaking, but knew she had to take the lead. It was her task to build the bridge between the skaters and the city. Soon, architect Terry Ledesky was on board to design the park. A bigger challenge was getting the city to supply the land. Sarah created a petition and gathered signatures from skaters, parents, teachers, and even police officers. She then led a group of 40 young people to address the city council. She pointed out that the city already maintained a swimming pool, baseball fields, and other public recreational facilities. Why not a skate park?

The council's major concern was the cost of liability insurance. This insurance would help protect the city in case it was sued by an injured skater. Nobody Special researched and reported on how other communities with skate parks dealt with this issue through rules, warning signs, and other measures. This helped calm the city council's concerns. The city finally agreed to supply land near the city swimming pool. Sarah and the skaters launched a fundraising effort to turn the dream into concrete.

The Oak Harbor skate park opened in 1998. To make it real, it took Sarah Swagart—a Third Sider—to help bridge the differences between skaters and the city.

CREATING A THIRD SIDE

In Ury's view of conflict management, a third side can aim for one of three goals. Which goal it decides upon depends on what stage the conflict has reached. The first goal is prevention. Prevention tries to ease tensions before they turn into a power struggle. Second, there is resolution. Resolution involves efforts to keep a power struggle from growing into open conflict. The third goal is containment. Containment seeks to control the conflict after it breaks out. It works to keep an open conflict from turning destructive, or to keep an already destructive conflict from spreading.

For people who see a conflict simmering or ready to explode, one of the most frustrating feelings is of not knowing what to do. Often, people remain stuck as bystanders. Ury, though, describes 10 specific roles people can take on to assist in preventing, resolving, or containing a conflict. Combined, these "spider webs" can halt a destructive conflict.

When a conflict can still be prevented, Third Siders can choose to become:

* Providers, who share resources or knowledge, or offer respect or a sense of security
* Teachers, who teach tolerance, problem solving, or a new way to act during a conflict
* Bridge builders, who, like Sarah Swagart, help build relationships and create joint projects that bring together the people in a dispute

When a conflict has already turned into a power struggle, Third Siders can choose to become:

* Mediators, who can bring people together and help ease communication between the two sides
* Arbiters, who can use their authority to encourage negotiation, promote fairness, and make a judgment that both sides can follow

* Equalizers, who can use their power to even the playing field if one side is more powerful than the other
* Healers, who can listen and support the people involved in order to soothe hurt feelings that might cause a conflict to reignite

When open conflict is on the verge of erupting, or has already broken out, then containment is the goal. Third Siders can try to contain conflict by becoming:

* Witnesses, who detect warning signals and sound the alarm when a conflict is about to erupt
* Referees, who can establish rules that can keep conflict from worsening and spreading
* Peacekeepers, who can control a conflict by separating the people in the dispute, providing protection, and promoting helpful communication

Often in conflicts, two opponents can become blinded to any other opinion but their own. In contrast, Third Siders can see the bigger picture. "From this third perspective, the truth of each competing point of view can be appreciated," says Ury. "Shared interests often come to loom larger than the differences. People remember that they all, in the end, belong to the same extended community."

CONTAGIOUS CONFLICT AND THE CEASEFIRE PROGRAM

Preventing and resolving conflicts and power struggles are tough enough. Once conflicts turn violent, though, the need to bring them under control becomes more urgent—and more difficult. Lives may hang in the balance. Research suggests that violent conflicts tend to expand and grow worse if people ignore them.

CONFLICTS OVER RESOURCES VS. CONFLICTS OVER VALUES

Most conflicts fall into two broad categories: conflicts about resources, things such as land, water, and money; and conflicts about values, involving competing beliefs. Each category presents its unique challenges.

Generally, conflicts over resources are easier to solve. The different sides can usually reach a compromise about how to use the resource. Different soccer teams might negotiate a schedule for using the same practice field, for instance. Commonly used examples of resource conflicts are those between environmentalists and loggers about forest use, between employers and workers over pay and working conditions, and between countries as they compete for oil, water, and other natural resources.

Values conflicts are trickier to solve and often more intense. They involve beliefs about right and wrong. People involved in values conflicts often have strong emotions and beliefs tied to their

An example of a values conflict is the one between abortion (pro-choice) supporters and antiabortion advocates. In 1993, opposing demonstrators stood side-by-side outside the U.S. Supreme Court in Washington, D.C., where the court was hearing arguments about whether a federal law could be used by abortion supporters to sue protestors who block women's access to abortion clinics.

(continues)

(continued)

positions. They tend to see the issue in strict terms: Their side is completely right, and the other side is completely wrong. They may view the other side's position as a personal attack against them. Communication between the two sides is often distrustful and testy, if it occurs at all. Familiar examples of values conflicts pit gun control advocates against gun rights activists, abortion rights supporters against anti-abortion advocates, and fundamentalist religious groups against "nonbelievers."

Resource conflicts and values conflicts require very different approaches. Resolving resource conflicts may rely more on logic and practical solutions. Values conflicts may require more effort in regards to emotional and psychological understanding. Both kinds of conflict benefit from expressions of mutual respect and tolerance, but these positive attitudes play especially important roles when dealing with values disputes.

Gary Slutkin is a doctor at the University of Illinois at Chicago. His specialty is epidemiology, the study of how disease and infections spread. He has studied the spread of tuberculosis, cholera, and human immunodeficiency virus (HIV) in Africa and the United States. In 1995, Slutkin had a new idea. He noticed that violence seemed to act like a contagious disease, spreading between people. If someone has a cold or flu, he or she may transmit the illness to another person. Slutkin wondered if a violent act could transmit violence to others. For example, if a person beat up someone else, would the victim or his or her friends become "infected" and strike back or attack someone else? If others got involved, would they be more likely to use violence themselves?

Slutkin decided to address violence as though it were a public health crisis, a form of a deadly disease. In many ways, it is: Murder is the top killer of teens and young adults in major cities. Slutkin founded the Chicago Center for Violence Prevention and began the CeaseFire program.

The goal of CeaseFire is to block the spread of violence in two ways. First, it tries to interrupt cycles of shootings. For example, if one gang attacks another, then the other side is likely to hit back with violence. This often leads to back-and-forth revenge shootings. CeaseFire's main purpose is to stop this from happening. Second, the program wants to get people to practice healthier behaviors. In violent neighborhoods, many young people grow up thinking violence is an acceptable way to deal with conflict. Slutkin compares this part of the program to an anti-smoking campaign—only instead of empowering people to give up cigarettes, it works with people to give up guns and violence. The program tries to convince people to choose nonviolent options in response to conflict. CeaseFire also helps children stay out or get out of gangs.

CeaseFire hires former gang members to help with its activities. Most of these former gang members have spent time in prison. Called "violence interrupters," these men and women know how to find out what is going on in a neighborhood. Even though they are now law-abiding citizens, their history means that gang members know and respect them. "We helped create the madness, and now we're trying to debug it," one interrupter told a reporter.

Through their contacts on the street, violence interrupters find out who is angry enough to shoot an enemy. They then move fast to set up a meeting with the potential shooter to talk them out of it. "The interrupters have to deal with how to get someone to save face," Slutkin told *The New York Times.* "In other words, how do you not do a shooting if someone has insulted you, if all of your friends are expecting you to do that? . . . In fact, what our interrupters do is put social pressure in the other direction." If someone does get shot, members of the CeaseFire crew show up at the hospital in an attempt to stop any retaliation. Their job is not to turn in criminals to the police. Instead, the interrupters focus on stopping a vengeful act. They want to stop the "infection" of violence from spreading.

CONNIE RICE:
SPEAKING TRUTH TO POWER

Connie Rice seems to have played every Third Sider role—equalizer, teacher, mediator, and many more. This Los Angeles civil rights lawyer has battled for decades to get fairer treatment for the city's poor and disadvantaged.

By age 18, Rice realized that she wanted to practice law to fight injustice. She graduated from Harvard University in 1978 and won a scholarship to New York University School of Law. She also earned her black belt in tae kwon do, an accomplishment of which she is especially proud.

Rice moved to Los Angeles in 1991 to work for the NAACP Legal Defense Fund. She represented the Bus Riders Union, a community organization that sued the Metropolitan Transit Authority for not doing enough to provide public transportation in the poorer parts of the city. She won and got more resources put into those bus routes. Rice also took on the Los Angeles Police Department. Her office sued the department, accusing police officers of abuse of black, Latino, and other minority suspects. Again, her side won. Since then, though, she has frequently partnered with the police to help them reduce abuses. She has worked with them to find ways of improving relations with the community.

Rice's efforts focus on helping the underdog. She challenges whatever city office, department, or group she feels is neglecting or threatening a particular community. She is a fierce opponent of criminal gangs, but she will work with gang members to bring about positive change. "I always begin with the question, 'Who has the power to change this?'" Rice said in an interview with the magazine *The Sun*. "When it comes to police reform, it's the police. With gangs, it's the gang members and

CeaseFire has produced good results in Chicago. One study found that shootings in neighborhoods in which Cease-Fire works dropped between 16 percent and 27 percent.

their communities. I need to ally myself with the people who can solve the problem."

Rice has won dozens of community awards for her work. Along the way, she has had to confront friends and foes alike in her campaigns for fairness and justice. "I've been suing my friends for 20 years," she said. "But when you know the people in power, you still have to be a burr under their saddle and demand change, because power concedes nothing without a demand."

Civil rights attorney Connie Rice—cousin of former Secretary of State Condoleezza Rice—has focused her career on helping Los Angeles's poor and disadvantaged. Here, she speaks during funeral services for attorney Johnnie L. Cochran Jr. in 2005.

Similar neighborhoods where CeaseFire was not active did not see such improvements. Other cities are now introducing anti-violence programs patterned after CeaseFire.

Slutkin believes that more police and longer prison sentences will do little to defuse violence, especially in the long run. Better solutions lie in changing reactions to conflict and changing community attitudes toward using violence. "Punishment doesn't drive behavior," Slutkin says. "Copying and modeling and the social expectations of your peers [are] what drive your behavior."

CHECKS AND BALANCES IN THE UNITED STATES

6

Ambition must be made to counteract ambition.

—James Madison (1751–1836), former U.S. president and principle author of the U.S. Constitution

Encouraging conflict would seem to go against common sense. Logically, conflict would seem to hurt the harmony and productivity that most people and groups want. Conflict, though, can be more than an obstacle to progress. It can also serve as a brake on bad ideas, unthinking behavior, and corrupt leadership. That was the conclusion reached by James Madison, often called the "father of the U.S. Constitution." He proposed building conflict into the blueprint for the new U.S. government. It took the form of various "checks and balances." It was a revolutionary idea that remains at work today.

In 1776, the British colonies along the East Coast of North America declared independence from Great Britain. In 1781, colonial troops defeated the British at Yorktown, the last major battle of the Revolutionary War. British and colonial

73

representatives signed the Treaty of Paris two years later, officially ending the war.

The following four years proved to be tough for the new nation—the United States of America. The leaders of the states distrusted one another and were reluctant to cooperate with each other and the national government, called the Congress of the Confederation. The congress had little structure or strength to get things done. It struggled to collect the tax money it needed from state governments in order to do its work.

The national government was largely powerless when, between 1786 and 1787, an armed uprising of farmers broke out in western Massachusetts. They were protesting taxes that were costing some of them their land and property. Known as Shays' Rebellion, it was soon put down by the Massachusetts militia. George Washington, John Adams, and other national leaders feared it was a sign of conflicts to come. The country, they believed, needed a stronger central government to prevent such threats.

That idea, though, made many people nervous in the new country. It had only recently escaped the heavy hands of Great Britain and King George III. Would that strict leadership now be replaced with a new version? What would prevent the creation of a new governing class? What would stop the rise of corrupt and greedy leaders, abusive laws, and the chipping away of hard-won rights and freedoms?

In May 1787, leaders from the different states gathered in Philadelphia. They would spend the next four months debating a national constitution. James Madison stepped into the center of this political storm. Less than five-and-a-half feet tall (about 1.65 meters) and slight of build, he was not very intimidating. He was, however, a giant of a political thinker. He had more to do with crafting the U.S. Constitution—and thus, the structure of the U.S. government—than any other individual.

Madison believed that people are naturally self-centered, or concerned mainly with their own well-being. This leads to

James Madison planned for a way to resolve conflicts when he proposed a system of checks and balances for the U.S. government. In this painting, Madison is shown sitting directly in front of President George Washington as he signs the U.S. Constitution in 1787.

conflicts when groups go after their own goals at the expense of others. Madison suggested the creation of a system that would use competition and constructive conflict to control such groups. In a sense, he proposed fighting conflict with conflict.

A SYSTEM OF CHECKS AND BALANCES

Madison presented two strategies for limiting government power. First, he pushed for the creation of a far-reaching national government to bind the different states under one federation. This larger government would have the size and strength to stop destructive groups that might try to take over power.

The government would feature "a greater variety of inter-ests, of pursuits, of passions, which check each other," Madi-son argued. In other words, more groups bound together in such a republic would be more likely to confront destructive groups. This structure would keep wild grabs at power from succeeding. At the same time, certain powers were to be left to the states. This would provide an additional check against the power of the federal government.

Second, Madison and others proposed creating the federal government with three parts, or branches. These branches included the Executive (the president and executive depart-ments), Legislative (Congress—specifically the Senate and House of Representatives), and Judicial (the federal courts and legal system). In addition to its own regular tasks, each branch would have methods for limiting the power of the other two branches.

The Constitutional Convention adopted the new U.S. Con-stitution on September 17, 1787. It was ratified by the states and went into effect on June 21, 1788. The Bill of Rights—the first 10 amendments to the Constitution—was added in 1789. These amendments guaranteed individual rights, including the freedom of speech and religion, the right to be protected from unreasonable searches by the authorities, the right to a trial by a jury, and the banning of "cruel and unusual punish-ment." These rights offered other tools for citizens to protect themselves from government actions.

James Madison did not get everything he wished for inserted into the U.S. Constitution, but its plans for limiting government power by managing conflict has proved to be a work of genius. Often, critics complain that certain checks and balances make government slow and inefficient. The rules may make it difficult or time-consuming to take action on important issues. On the other hand, as U.S. President Harry S. Truman said, "Whenever you have an efficient government you have a dictatorship." At its best, constructive conflict keeps a country's leaders honest and its citizens alert.

THE ADVERSARIAL SYSTEM

Conflict management is also built into U.S. courts. Called the adversarial system, this process pits two sides in a case against each other. In a criminal case, a lawyer for the prosecution presents the evidence against suspects. A defense lawyer may help suspects defend themselves. Civil cases involve lawsuits rather than criminal charges. The two sides argue and debate. A judge or jury listens, and then makes a ruling based on the evidence.

The Bill of Rights guarantees U.S. citizens the right to a trial by jury. The jury, a group of the defendant's peers, analyzes the evidence while a judge referees the proceedings. Most criminal and civil cases in the United States, though, are settled without a trial. The court may dismiss the charges, a suspect may plead guilty and accept a sentence, or the parties in a civil case may agree to a settlement out of court.

The adversarial system has a noteworthy fault. Some outcomes may have more to do with money than with truth and justice. Constructive conflict can be difficult to manage if one side has more resources and better skills. A defendant, for example, can be at a big disadvantage if she or he cannot afford a good lawyer.

There was a time when penniless suspects had little choice but to defend themselves. Most were uneducated and knew nothing about law. This left them at the mercy of the court. A man named Clarence Earl Gideon helped to change that.

Gideon was no angel. He was a drifter with a criminal history. In 1961, he was arrested and charged with breaking into a pool hall in Panama City, Florida. He asked for a lawyer to defend him. The judge denied his request. Gideon argued that he was innocent, but a jury convicted him. He was sentenced to five years in prison.

From his prison cell, Gideon researched the law. Then he wrote directly to the U.S. Supreme Court. He specifically cited the part of the Sixth Amendment that says: "In all criminal

Denied an attorney by the state of Florida and imprisoned for burglary, Clarence Earl Gideon researched and argued for his constitutional right to have an attorney. In the 1963 *Gideon v. Wainwright* decision, the U.S. Supreme Court ruled that anyone accused of a crime has a right to an attorney.

prosecutions, the accused shall enjoy the right . . . to have the Assistance of Counsel for his defense." He also referred to the Fourteenth Amendment that applies this right to state courts.

The Supreme Court agreed to hear Gideon's case. In March 1963, it ruled in his favor, saying: "The right of one charged with crime to counsel may not be deemed fundamental and essential to fair trials in some countries, but it is in ours." Gideon was appointed a lawyer and his case was retried. This time he was found not guilty.

Out of this legal ruling grew a system of public defenders. These are lawyers whom the court appoints to represent defendants if the defendants cannot afford their own counsel. "It really is startling to think that . . . someone could be sent to prison without counsel," said Kate Jones of the National Association of Criminal Defense Lawyers in a 2003 interview to the Associated Press. "Whatever his personal history, Gideon was very persistent and courageous in raising this important constitutional issue. It's a remarkable story and shows how much one person can affect change."

There are still traces of inequality in the legal system. Studies suggest that court-appointed lawyers in many states are inexperienced, overworked, and struggling to represent defendants effectively. "There was a gap between our great hope and what was realized," Abe Krash told *The New York Times* 40 years after Gideon went to the Supreme Court. Krash was one of the lawyers who worked on Gideon's case. "It is simply not sufficient to say you're entitled to a lawyer. You have to have a lawyer who is competent and experienced in trying criminal cases. Equally important, the lawyer who is appointed has to have the resources available to adequately defend the case."

The adversarial system and constructive conflict work best when the "fight" is fair. When one side has major advantages in money and other resources, however, it has a much better chance of winning the conflict.

ECONOMIC CONFLICT AND LABOR DISPUTES

Economic conflicts often follow an adversarial pattern, too. Economies, such as the one in the United States, rely on competition among companies to control prices. If one business charges too much, another may start charging less for the same product or service. In this way, the second business will likely attract the first business's customers. That will in turn force the first business to lower prices to get its customers back. Competition also drives creativity. A company can do better than its competitors if it can create a better product than theirs.

Labor disputes between a company's management and its workers represent another example of economic conflict. Workers may be convinced that they are underpaid, for instance. In other words, they feel they are not getting their fair share of a company's profits or other resources. Meanwhile, company owners and managers might not have the money or resources to give, or they may have other purposes for that money.

If workers feel that management is not being fair, they may go on strike. By stopping work, they seek to force management to offer a deal—usually more pay or better working conditions. In this way, workers and management act as opponents. The workers argue for what they feel is fair for them. Management battles for what the company wants and needs. If all goes well, the two sides work out a deal that both can accept.

A famous example of such a labor dispute was the Delano grape strike in the 1960s. Farm workers, many of them Latino and Filipino, performed the hard work of picking grapes and other produce. Grape pickers earned very little—$1.20 an hour and 10 cents for each basket of grapes picked, on average.

During the 1965 harvest, grape growers around Delano, California, cut the pay rates of these farm workers. The growers wanted to keep more of their profits for themselves

Cesar Chavez (*holding sign*) pickets with about 400 people at a Seattle supermarket in 1969 to peacefully protest grape farmers during the Delano grape strike, a labor dispute between grape pickers and farmers.

and their businesses. Upset, about half of the farm workers stopped work and went on strike. Among Spanish speakers, the strike became known as *La Causa*—the Cause. The grape growers, of course, still needed to get the grapes picked and trucked to grocery stores. They would lose millions of dollars if the grapes rotted in the fields, but they were unwilling to pay higher wages to the pickers. Therefore, the growers brought in workers from other states to do the picking.

The strikers responded with nonviolent protests. They marched and picketed near the fields. They tried to convince the replacement workers to quit. Growers brought in police to keep order and to intimidate the strikers. Officers arrested thousands for trespassing and fought with some strikers in the process.

Labor organizer and former farm worker Cesar Chavez emerged as the leader of the strike. Chavez and other leaders representing the farm workers challenged the growers with a new approach. In addition to stopping work, they publicized their cause around the United States. They formed alliances with students and religious leaders. Supporters stood outside grocery stores and told customers, "Help the farm workers by not buying grapes." More than 14 million people around the country joined the California grape boycott.

During the strike and boycott, California grape growers lost an estimated 20 percent to 25 percent of their income. Some faced bankruptcy. In 1969, the grape growers finally gave in to the workers' demands. The farm workers won new contracts that raised wages and improved working conditions in the fields.

DESTRUCTIVE CONFLICT IN THE UNITED STATES: THE CIVIL WAR

The Republican and Democratic parties are the two main groups that face off against each other in U.S. politics. They propose different policies and plans and then seek voter

CESAR CHAVEZ (1927–1993)

The work of labor leader Cesar Chavez went beyond the struggle for better pay and working conditions for farm workers. He also challenged the racism faced by Mexican Americans and other ethnic groups in the United States. Many white-owned businesses treated Latinos as second-class citizens. "No Dogs or Mexicans Allowed" was a common sign around Delano, California, in the 1940s.

In 1943, when he was 17, Chavez was arrested after he purposely sat in the "whites only" section of his local movie theater in Delano. According to the biography *Cesar Chavez: A Triumph of Spirit*, the

(continues)

Labor leader and civil rights activist Cesar Chavez (*center, facing camera*) testifies during a U.S. Senate Migrant Labor Subcommittee hearing in Sacramento, California, in 1966. Chavez often took the lead in negotiating and speaking on behalf of migrant workers.

(continued)

experience changed him: "Cesar learned that segregation was an evil, making people feel excluded and inferior. As a result, one of the main tenets of his later organizing philosophy was that neither racial nor ethnic prejudice had a place within a farm workers' union movement."

In 1952, Chavez began learning about the uses of nonviolent protest during conflicts. He built this strategy into campaigns for farm worker rights. Later on in the struggles, he also fasted, refusing to eat for days at a time. This not only demonstrated his dedication to the cause, it brought media attention to the struggle for equal rights.

Chavez died in 1993. In 1994, President Bill Clinton honored his memory with the Presidential Medal of Freedom. This award is the highest civilian honor a U.S. citizen can receive. Several states also celebrate Cesar Chavez Day every March 31 to recognize his life's work for fair treatment of all people.

approval to help put them into action. Each party may speak harshly as it argues its position and tears down the policies of the other side. At their best, these opponents work in service of the greater good of the country. Like watchdogs, they also keep an eye on each other, looking for bad behavior and corruption.

In government and politics, checks and balances and the adversarial system cannot always prevent destructive conflict. At times, the issues are so sensitive and explosive that they overwhelm thoughtful discussion, negotiation and resolution.

That was the case in the run-up to the U.S. Civil War. A long-simmering dispute was ready to erupt into the most destructive conflict the country has ever known. By the 1850s, tensions between Northern and Southern states had reached a boiling point. The two regions had been developing along very different lines. The North's economy relied more and more on factories and manufacturing. The South's economy, in contrast, had stayed largely built around farm production. This was mostly because of the labor of millions of black slaves who worked on farms and cotton plantations. The South's wealth and economy depended on this slave labor.

For decades, slavery had been a source of conflict between the two regions of the United States. Southern leaders wanted national policies that supported slavery. Northern leaders wanted national laws that benefited their own needs and interests. As the country expanded westward, this competition intensified. The South wanted new states to permit slavery. More slave states would give them more power in the federal government in Washington, D.C.

In the 1850s, the people of Fort Scott, Kansas, experienced the violent conflict of Bleeding Kansas, a time of unrest between those fighting for Kansas to be a slave state and those fighting for it to be a free state.

Northern leaders, however, wanted slavery banned in new states because it would protect their interests.

For a while, the two sides negotiated compromises. The Missouri Compromise of 1820 created the states of Missouri and Maine. It also banned slavery in states created from the former Louisiana Territory that stood north of latitude 36°, 30 minutes. The new state of Missouri was the one exception. In the Compromise of 1850, California was admitted to the United States as a free state. At the same time, the compromise tried to deal with slavery in other territories taken from Mexico in the Mexican-American War (1846–1848). The solution was to allow each state to decide for itself. Since most of this land was south of the line drawn by the Missouri Compromise, this solution did not cause much fuss in the North.

The Kansas-Nebraska Act of 1854 was a different story. This territory, which would become the states of Kansas and Nebraska, sat north of the Missouri Compromise line. The Compromise of 1850, however, had given the governments of new states the right to choose whether or not they would allow slavery. This went against the Missouri Compromise, and set off a fierce and sometimes bloody competition. Which side—free or slave—would gain a foothold in the newly settled West?

These events also led to the rapid rise of the Republican Party. For 20 years, the two principal political parties in the country had been the Democrats and Whigs. Then, the Kansas-Nebraska Act led to widespread revolt among Northern members of these two parties. Many banded together under a new political banner: the Republicans. By 1859, the organization had also included members of what was called the Know-Nothing Party. The principle that unified the Republican Party was the prevention of slavery's spread. Republicans dreaded the possibility that Southern slave states would grow in power and dominate the federal government. Southern Democrats held similar fears about their Northern foes.

The two regions heaped scorn on each other in ever increasing amounts. This criticism quickly turned into insults, as often happens in angry conflict. Southerners blasted Northerners as unprincipled, greedy, and stupid. Northerners returned the favor by calling Southerners backward, immoral, and cruel. Needless to say, these exchanges did not calm tensions.

In 1860 the Republicans nominated Abraham Lincoln for president. Lincoln, an Illinois lawyer and former Whig, was a well-spoken opponent of slavery. He reluctantly accepted slavery's existence in the South, but opposed its spread. Southerners feared his views because if slavery could not spread, the South's political and economic power would be snuffed out. Before long the South would be at a great political disadvantage if only free states were added. Southern Democrats called for a swift withdrawal of slave states from the Union if Lincoln were elected.

Lincoln was elected in November 1860. In his inaugural speech on March 4, 1861, he tried to calm war fever. He reassured slave states that they had nothing to fear from his administration. "We are not enemies, but friends," Lincoln said. "We must not be enemies. Though passion may have strained, it must not break our bonds of affection. The mystic chords of memory, stretching from every battlefield and patriot grave to every living heart and hearthstone all over this broad land, will yet swell the chorus of the Union, when again touched, as surely they will be, by the better angels of our nature."

Unfortunately, though, the conflict had passed the point of no return. Seven Southern states had already seceded from the Union before Lincoln gave that speech. Four more would soon join them. On April 12, 1861, Southern cannons fired the first shots of the Civil War.

Could the most destructive conflict in U.S. history have been avoided? Historians have been asking that question ever since the war's end.

DR. MARTIN LUTHER KING JR. AND NONVIOLENT PROTEST

The Civil War brought an end to slavery, but blacks continued to suffer social, legal, and economic discrimination in the United States, especially in the South. Their struggle to gain civil rights was often met with racist hate and violence.

In the 1950s, a new leader emerged with a strategy for changing the terms of this conflict. Dr. Martin Luther King Jr. recognized that blacks could never bring about change by force. Violence in pursuit of equal rights would only lead to a crushing defeat and more violence. "The ultimate weakness of violence is that it is a descending spiral, begetting the very thing it seeks to destroy," King said. "Instead of diminishing evil, it multiplies it . . . Through violence you may murder the hater, but you do not murder hate. In fact, violence merely increases hate. . . . Returning violence for violence multiplies violence, adding deeper darkness to a night already devoid of stars. Darkness cannot drive out hate; only love can do that."

A better alternative, King reasoned, involved nonviolent protest. He studied the methods of Indian leader Mohandas (Mahatma) Gandhi, who had used nonviolent protest to help win India's independence from Great Britain in the 1940s. Nonviolent protest confronts injustice with determined but peaceful opposition. When met with violence, nonviolent protestors do not fight back, even though they may be arrested or beaten.

During the civil rights movement of the 1950s and 1960s King's strategy exposed the brutal and hateful face of racism and bigotry. Protestors marched through city streets and were attacked with dogs and clubs. They were insulted and assaulted as they protested lunch counters that refused to serve blacks. Leaders and those who tried to

After the Kansas-Nebraska Act in 1854, it is difficult to see how the situation could have been resolved without bloodshed. According to conflict expert Morton Deutsch, five

Inspired by Gandhi, civil rights leader Dr. Martin Luther King Jr. used nonviolent protest to face conflict. Here, King speaks to protestors of an all-white Mississippi delegation at the Democratic National Convention in Atlantic City, New Jersey, in 1964.

help the cause were attacked and some were murdered. King himself was killed by a sniper in 1968.

Slowly, though, the courage of the protestors and the viciousness of the racists raised the awareness of Americans of all backgrounds. Eventually, laws were passed that protected the rights that had been denied to blacks for a century.

developments are common among situations that turn into destructive conflict:

* Distrustful, unreliable, and bad communication between parties in the conflict
* The belief that the only solution is if one side "wins"
* Goals that focus on building up power while beating down the opposition
* Hostile attitudes that worsen and grow, increasing touchiness about differences, and an unwillingness to recognize common ground
* Misjudgments and misperceptions that feed the conflict's growth

All of these features were at work in the run-up to the Civil War.

The U.S. Civil War lasted more than four years, and left more than 600,000 dead and 400,000 wounded. Many Southern states suffered widespread devastation. That was the cost of the destructive conflict that put the United States back together and freed more than 4 million people from slavery.

As the Union victory in the war became certain, President Lincoln created plans to treat the defeated South with generosity and respect. Then, Lincoln was assassinated on April 14, 1865. His successor, Andrew Johnson, did not have the political power or skills to follow through on Lincoln's vision. Instead, Republican congressional leaders pushed through policies to punish the South. During the period known as Reconstruction, Union troops were stationed throughout Southern states. Southern leaders were shown little consideration or respect. At the same time, the Republicans were slow to provide aid to help the South rebuild.

History suggests that resentment is almost always a result of violent, destructive conflict, whatever the outcome. Many white Southerners were left with bitter feelings after their region's defeat and the loss of their way of life. They resented the overbearing rule from the Republican-controlled govern- ment. They resented that former slaves were now legally considered their equals. For nearly a century afterwards, Southern states voted against the Republican Party. Southern whites' unwavering support of Democrats earned the region the political nickname of "The Solid South."

This loyalty flipped in the 1960s as the policies of Demo- crats and Republicans changed. Northern Democrats increas- ingly supported laws that protected the civil rights of blacks, which angered many Southern Democrats. Partly in response, Republican leaders developed a "pro-South" and anti-black political strategy to regain power that the party had lost in the Great Depression in the 1930s. This history has contributed to bitter feelings that continue to fuel distrust between many Democrats and Republicans.

MANAGING CONFLICTS AROUND THE WORLD

If you want to make peace, you don't talk to your friends. You talk to your enemies.

—Moshe Dayan (1915–1981)
Israeli general and politician

In 1948, Israel was founded in the heart of the Middle East. With the help of the United Nations, it was created as a Jewish state in its people's historic homeland. European Jews had only recently suffered horrible crimes and genocide during World War II (1939–1945). Genocide is the planned murder of people with the goal of destroying a racial, ethnic, or religious group. In their own country, Jews hoped to be safe in their unity and strength.

However, Israel was formed from lands that were already populated by Palestinian Arabs. The conflict between Palestinian Arabs and Israeli Jews turned destructive almost immediately. Over time, hundreds of thousands of Palestinian Arabs fled Israel as neighboring Arab countries, including

A rocket fired from the Gaza strip hit the city center of Ashkelon, Israel, in February 2009, as children were walking to school. Palestinian sympathizers have launched rockets into Israeli neighborhoods for many years, which continues to deepen Israeli frustration and anger in the Israeli-Palestinian conflict.

Egypt, Jordan, and Syria, attacked Israel, trying to destroy the new country. Other Palestinians were forced from their homes by Israel's police and military. During the next 25 years, Arab and Israeli forces went to war several more times.

In addition, Palestinian terrorists carried out deadly violence against Israeli soldiers and civilians. The Israelis responded with attacks against Palestinian militants that also killed civilians. The Israeli military has periodically invaded and occupied Palestinian territories to try to stop these terrorist attacks.

As the years passed, Israel grew in economic and military strength. In contrast, the Palestinian territories—dominated by Israel—crumbled. Resentments grew, back-and-forth attacks continued, and fear and distrust between Israelis and Palestinians escalated. On many occasions, diplomatic efforts have tried to ease tensions and guide the two sides toward peace. Hopeful moments have come and gone, but the two sides have become locked in an intractable conflict.

THE NATURE OF INTRACTABLE CONFLICTS

An intractable conflict is a serious dispute that is difficult to resolve, often because it has been going on for a long time. These kinds of conflicts rarely respond to common resolution strategies such as negotiation and mediation. "In some cases, this is because the conflict itself is not 'ripe' for resolution," explains Professor Diana Chigas, a conflict resolution scholar at Tufts University, in a 2003 report for the Conflict Information Consortium. "[I]n other words, one or both parties may not have strong motives to de-escalate because they believe the costs of working to de-escalate or solve the conflict exceed the benefits. Even when de-escalation would be beneficial, a society may be too divided to permit bold initiatives for de-escalation, or the conflict may be intertwined with other regional or global conflicts."

Professor Chigas explains that most intractable conflicts share three characteristics:

* They involve basic human needs and values that the people involved feel are "critical to their survival" and cannot be negotiated.
* The threat seems so dire that it affects all parts of people's lives.
* Intractable conflict tends to escalate and fuel itself. The two sides paint each other as evil, untrustworthy, and less than human. At the same time,

they think of their own side as acting honorably and courageously in the face of the threat. Almost everything that happens is interpreted through these beliefs. This effect, Chigas says, destroys trust and prevents each side from understanding the other.

The Israeli-Palestinian conflict exhibits these symptoms of intractable conflict. First, both sides point to "basic human needs and values" that they feel unable to negotiate. Many Israeli Jews—with their painful history and past wars with Arab countries—have a powerful fear for the survival of their people and their nation. Many Palestinians—having lost

Israeli officials ordered a wall built between Israel and sections of the Palestinian-controlled West Bank to protect their citizens from attacks by Palestinian terrorists. The barrier has also restricted Palestinian access to jobs, hospitals, and resources, as well as family and friends, on the other side of the wall.

much of their land and freedom—hold weak hopes for a better future.

Second, the "experience of threat" by both Israelis and Palestinians has lodged itself deeply into the two cultures and communities. Some Palestinian cities frequently experience shortages of food, medicine, and other needs. Israel severely limits where and when Palestinian Arabs can travel. For Israelis, some areas are vulnerable to rocket attacks by Palestinian militants. Palestinian terrorists with bombs have targeted restaurants and shops in Israel, killing Israeli civilians.

Third, intractable conflict goes through cycles of escalation in words and actions. Israelis and Palestinians regularly trade threats, insults, and poor treatment. As examples, compare the angry statements of religious leaders Dr. Ahmad Abu Halabiya, a Palestinian, and Rabbi Yaacov Perrin, of Israel:

> Halabiya in 2000: "Have no mercy on the Jews, no matter where they are, in any country. Fight them, wherever you are. Wherever you meet them, kill them . . ."

> Perrin in 1994: "One million Arabs are not worth a Jewish fingernail."

Such spiteful language helps enemies excuse brutal behavior toward each other. If the enemy is inhuman or evil, the other side believes that brutality is acceptable, even praiseworthy. Not surprisingly, such words and attitudes destroy trust and effective communication between the two sides. They serve to escalate the conflict.

One might think that people involved in an intractable conflict might tire of the destructive results. There are extremists, though, who gain power from keeping the conflict going. They encourage people's anger or even launch new attacks in hopes of triggering a destructive response. Extremists find recruits for their cause among despairing people and those nursing their own grudges. "What is objectionable, what is dangerous, about extremists is not that they are extreme, but that they are intolerant," said politician Robert F. Kennedy. "The evil is not what they say about their cause, but what they say about their opponents." Kennedy, who served as a U.S. senator from New York, U.S. attorney general, and a presidential candidate, was himself murdered by an anti-Israel extremist in 1968.

How then can the world hope to solve intractable conflicts? The truth is that these disputes present enormous challenges. There is no quick fix. Relations between longtime enemies require mending and peacemaking on many levels. An intractable conflict is like a deep wound. Only with skill, attention, patience, determination, and time can such a conflict begin to heal. Even minor stumbles can tear it open again.

GLOBALIZATION AND DIPLOMACY

People in suits shuffle papers while sitting around a big table. Small flags indicate which country each representative serves. This has been a traditional image of diplomacy, the management of communication and relations between nations. That image, though, is changing. In the past, interactions among governments have mostly featured official contacts between government diplomats. Globalization has been changing this.

Globalization is the spread of social and economic connections around the world. It has greatly increased the exchange of business, communication, and ideas between people of every nation and culture. Children in the United States wear T-shirts made in Vietnam, for example, while Vietnamese children watch movies made in the United States. The Internet allows bloggers around the world to rapidly share information and opinions. In many places, travelers can move between countries and cultures with little trouble.

When it comes to managing conflict, changes brought by globalization offer both opportunities and risks. Hazards include increased competition that can lead to abuse and more conflict. A rich country may buy a poor country's corn in order to make ethanol, which can be used—like gasoline—as fuel. Meanwhile, people in the poor country may not have enough to eat. International crime and terrorism are other dangers. Corrupt and destructive people can communicate destructive ideas and hatred more easily than ever before. Drug dealers and prostitution rings can run their illegal operations on a wider scale.

Improved global communication, though, also presents opportunities for better understanding and cooperation. Natural disasters illustrate this hopeful development. When catastrophe strikes, global communications can quickly get the word out and speed help. In December 2004, for example, a tsunami blasted coastlines in southern Asia. The tsunami and the flooding it caused killed more than 200,000 people. Because of global communications, international aid workers quickly rushed in to help. In just weeks, donors from around the world pitched in billions of dollars in relief.

Another plus is how the Internet and other resources make it easier to learn about other groups and cultures than ever before. "Education is the enemy of bigotry and hate," entertainer Barbara Streisand once said. "It is hard to hate someone you truly understand."

PREVENTIVE DIPLOMACY

People who study and work in conflict resolution have a saying: "You can build either a $50 fence at the top of a cliff, or a $50 million hospital at the bottom." In other words, it is easier to stop destructive conflict before it happens. The dispute will be much harder to manage once it "goes over the cliff" and causes destruction. It will then require spending a lot more effort and money—not to mention that it will cause more pain and suffering—to clean up the mess.

AMNESTY INTERNATIONAL: LETTERS TO THE RESCUE

In the early morning hours of April 26, 2005, 20 police moved in to capture Gagan Thapa in Kathmandu, Nepal. The former leader of the Nepal Student Union had been active in protesting for democracy and human rights in this Asian country. Earlier that year, King Gyanendra had taken over the government and declared emergency powers. Basic freedoms were suspended.

Thapa was given a 90-day detention order and jailed. He was charged with sedition—working to overthrow the king. Family and friends feared he

The attention of Amnesty International and people around the world encouraged Nepalese leaders to free Gagan Thapa, a student leader who was charged with sedition (inciting resistance to government authority) and imprisoned in Nepal.

might be beaten or abused. There was no way to guarantee his safety.

Then Amnesty International got involved. Amnesty International is a watchdog organization that monitors the treatment of political prisoners and other "prisoners of conscience" around the world. When a nonviolent activist is jailed, the organization sends out alerts to let people and the press know what has happened. The aim is to shine a spotlight

(continues)

(continued)

on a prisoner's situation. That puts pressure on the government to not abuse the person. In this way, a letter writer can confront injustice half a world away.

Amnesty International members wrote letters to Nepal's government, protesting Thapa's detention. He was released soon afterward. Thapa thanked Amnesty International for helping protect him. "If the international community had not been present at the right moment, the action taken against me would have been more serious . . . As soon as the international pressure started, the police changed their tone."

This is the philosophy behind a concept called preventive diplomacy. Preventive diplomacy works to keep a destructive conflict from turning violent. If violence has already started to spread, preventive diplomacy can be used to control it and deal with the root conflict.

An ethnic conflict in the African country of Rwanda demonstrates the need for preventive diplomacy. Relations between two ethnic groups in that country—the Hutus and the Tutsis—had been strained for many years. The two groups have a history of competing for power.

In early 1994, there were reports that the Hutu-controlled government was planning mass killings of Tutsis. In early April of that year, Rwanda's president, a Hutu, died when his plane was shot down. Tutsis were blamed for the attack. Soon afterward, Hutu militias began to regularly attack and murder Tutsis. Men, women, and children were shot, burned, and hacked to death.

The United Nations already had 2,000 armed soldiers to keep the peace on the ground in Rwanda. The soldiers' Canadian commander, General Roméo Dallaire, alerted the UN about the situation. He requested 2,000 additional troops. He believed that a force of 4,000 well-trained soldiers would be enough to stop the violence before it gained more momentum.

Representatives in the UN disagreed. They argued that a bigger force would only escalate the conflict. The UN Security Council denied Dallaire's request. It told General Dallaire to take no action except to defend his peacekeepers.

The conflict now raged out of control. In just 100 days, approximately 800,000 or more Tutsis were murdered. The killings ended after a Tutsi-led rebel army captured most of the country. Afterward, military experts examined the evidence. They agreed with General Dallaire: Early preven-

A young Tutsi refugee sits outside the Red Cross refugee camp of Nya-rushishi in Rwanda in 1994. The approximately 12,000 Tutsis living in that camp moved there to seek safety from Hutu militias and supporters of Rwanda's former government, who had massacred about 800,000 Tutsis during months of fighting that year.

tive action by a larger UN force could have stopped the mass killings.

Preventive diplomacy can take many forms. It can feature humanitarian action to provide food, medicine, and other supplies in a crisis. It can guide two opposing sides to put down their weapons so that each can trust that it will be safe from attack. Preventative diplomacy can even supply peace-keepers to keep enemies from fighting. The purpose of each of these actions is to build that fence along the top of the cliff. Such efforts can keep a conflict from going over the edge and leading to violence.

Getting that fence built can be a struggle. On the world stage, it is often difficult to get different countries to agree on how to use preventive diplomacy. For example, some countries may not view a situation as a crisis. Also, if the destructive conflict takes place within one country—as it did in Rwanda—other countries may be unwilling to interfere. Lastly, leaders may not want to supply money and other resources before a full-blown crisis erupts. It is usually easier to rally support and action once conflict turns violent. Countries, like people, are often more likely to deal with conflict only after it becomes an emergency.

PUTTING CONFLICT RESOLUTION SKILLS TO WORK

8

The most basic of all human needs is the need to understand and be understood. The best way to understand people is to listen to them.

—Ralph G. Nichols (1907–2005), communication scholar, University of Minnesota

Humans are social animals, just like wolves, apes, dolphins, and even ants. Humans rely on the support, teamwork, and love of other people. Chances are that a person would not last very long if he or she were abandoned to live alone on an island.

Negative conflict can wear at the bonds that hold relationships together. That is what makes conflict resolution skills so important. They are the tools people use to weave these connections and repair them when they fray.

Psychologists have found that the quality of people's lives is closely tied to their ability to manage conflict.

Conflict that does not find resolution erodes relationships with family members and friends. Destructive conflict within a group sucks valuable energy away from its teamwork and goals. Constructive conflict, on the other hand, can actually strengthen individuals and their relationships. It can also help empower the groups to which they belong.

STEPS FOR MANAGING CONFLICT RESOLUTION

Conflict and conflict resolution involve very complex issues. Understanding them requires knowledge of psychology, sociology, and law, as well as history and anthropology (the exploration of human development and culture). The subject of conflict has gained more attention in the last generation. Dozens of colleges and universities now offer degrees in peace and conflict studies. Training in conflict management is now a regular feature in many businesses and organizations.

Research has revealed new insights into the nature of conflict. One of the most fascinating traits that has been discovered is that very different conflicts share very similar features. This is true whether these conflicts occur at the interpersonal, community, or international level. A squabble between siblings in a sandbox may share similarities with a squabble between adult coworkers at the office, for example A dispute between neighbors about a shared fence may resemble a dispute between two countries about their shared border. Likewise, disputes at different levels may share similar steps toward resolution. A friend might apologize to try to make up for having done something mean. Nations may also apologize to address a past wrong.

In 2008, for example, Australia's Prime Minister Kevin Rudd apologized to his country's native people, the Aborigines. When the British colonized that continent in the 1800s, Aboriginal groups lost their way of life and most of their lands. They have struggled with poverty and social

In 2008, Australian Prime Minister Kevin Rudd (*left*) gave an official apology on behalf of all Australians for past treatment of Aborigines, who continue to feel the affects of past persecution. Here, Rudd talks with prominent Australian Aborigine Lowitja O'Donoghue after he delivered the apology.

problems ever since. Even more troubling, some 100,000 Aboriginal children—known as the Stolen Generations— were taken from their families. This history angered many Aborigines and strained relations between them and white Australians.

In his apology, the prime minister said, "For the pain, suffering, and hurt of these Stolen Generations, their descendants, and for their families left behind, we say sorry." He then vowed to help Aborigines improve their lives.

Research has helped identify the most effective strategies for dealing with conflict. The foundation for all of them is good communication. Good communication skills give people the means to express what they want and need. Perhaps more importantly, these skills allow people to listen for and understand what *others* want and need.

APOLOGY ACCEPTED

"I'm sorry."

Every toddler is taught to say these words when he or she has done something mean or wrong. Adults have also been relearning the value of a sincere apology. They are finding that saying "I'm sorry" can help defuse many conflicts in personal, business, legal, and social disputes.

The field of medicine is one area where apologies are being offered more often. When doctors make a mistake, they are often reluctant to admit it. They and their insurance companies have traditionally feared that such an admission could be used against them in a lawsuit. That thinking is changing. Medical professionals have found that a genuine apology often has the opposite effect.

Dr. Tapas K. Das Gupta had been a cancer surgeon for 40 years. In 2006, he accidentally removed the wrong rib from a patient, according to an article in *The New York Times*. He went to the woman, told her about his mistake, and said he was very sorry. The woman decided not to sue. "She told me that the doctor was completely candid, completely honest, and so frank that she and her husband—usually the husband wants to pound the guy—that all the anger was gone," her lawyer said. "His apology helped get the case settled for a lower amount of money."

To the surprise of some, hospitals that are open about their mistakes are finding that their honesty saves money. The University of Michigan

Good conflict management requires three core abilities:

※ **Emotional awareness and self-control:** The ability to recognize feelings and express them clearly requires practice. The ability to control anger is crucial to keeping the lines of communication open.

※ **Active listening and perspective taking:** Listening means more than hearing the words. Active listening requires showing attention and interest.

Health System reported that claims and lawsuits dropped from 262 in 2001 to 83 in 2007. This cut costs for legal defense and claims by two-thirds, *The New York Times* reported. Admitting mistakes also makes hospitals safer because problems are out in the open and can be corrected before they happen again.

Apologies are about more than just saying the magic words, though. A real apology is a kind of ritual with three parts, according to the directors of Mediation Matters, a Maryland-based company with members that serve as mediators between parties in disagreement. First, the person who did the harm must admit that she or he did something that caused hurt or injury. Second, the person must show genuine regret or shame about what happened. Third, the person must apologize without making excuses or in any way trying to justify his or her actions. In that way, they make themselves vulnerable to the person they hurt.

When appropriate, the offender should also attempt to make up for what she or he did. If the damage was a smashed window, for example, the guilty party might agree to fix it. As Desmond Tutu, the South African bishop and Nobel Peace Prize winner, said: "If you take my pen and say you are sorry, but don't give me the pen back, nothing has happened." Actions, whenever possible, should back up the words.

Perspective taking involves an honest investigation of the other side's concerns, wants, and needs.

❋ **Honest and thoughtful expression:** Expressing wants and needs in a conflict is a delicate balancing act. Thoughts and feelings need to be expressed honestly. At the same time, the language and tone used has a powerful effect on whether the message gets through.

EMOTIONAL AWARENESS AND SELF-CONTROL

Anger and fear can be proper emotional responses to a situation. These feelings let a person know that he or she is being treated badly and/or needs protection. Feelings can also give people the willpower to defend themselves or to right a wrong.

Being aware of one's emotions is important in managing conflict resolution. It is important to deal with feelings as well as actions when sorting through a dispute. If emotions are not addressed, there is a very good chance that the conflict will return. But that is not all. Like an infection that has been ignored, such emotions will often return with more destructive power.

Feelings during a conflict need to be handled with care. Anger is a very unstable emotion. It can lead to aggressive words and actions that can hurt people. It may also lead to a physical confrontation that can end in violence. When conflict turns aggressive—in words or actions—it is time to walk away or get help.

There are people, too, who have difficulty controlling their anger. They regularly respond aggressively to stressful situations. They may come across as bullies, and may start conflict where none is justified. These people may need outside help to learn how to control their anger.

In the long run, uncontrolled fear can result in as much damage as uncontrolled anger. Fear can cause people to run away from a conflict that needs to be handled. Running away may even turn a person into a victim as others take advantage of him or her. This can also allow a problem to worsen, making fear turn into resentment and anger.

Safety, though, is the most important thing to think about when a confrontation takes place. If a situation feels out of control, it is time to leave. This should be an automatic decision if drugs or alcohol are involved. Drugs and alcohol often lower the user's self-control. This greatly increases the chances for aggression and violence.

Emotional outbursts are likely to make a confrontation worse. Again, this can be the case whether the conflict is interpersonal or international. "Speak when you are angry—and you'll make the best speech you'll ever regret," says educator and writer Dr. Laurence J. Peter. Better to take a break, let tempers cool, and come back to the conflict later with calmer heads. It is still important to revisit the dispute and seek resolution, though, especially when it involves family and friends.

When managing conflict, people need to practice self-control of their voice and body language, too. Studies have found that more than 60 percent of communication between people is nonverbal. In other words, people pick up more about what a person is feeling and thinking from body language and tone of voice than from the words they actually speak. People might say all the right, diplomatic words, but scowls, crossed arms, shifting eyes, or sarcastic tones cast doubts on whether or not they mean what they say.

ACTIVE LISTENING AND PERSPECTIVE TAKING

"No set of skills is more important for negotiating than being a good listener," writes David W. Johnson and Roger T. Johnson in their book, *Reducing School Violence Through Conflict Resolution.* That is why active listening skills are an essential part of training for mediators and negotiators.

It can be very frustrating to speak to listeners who aren't really listening. Through facial expressions, body language, and other cues, they send the signals that they are not interested in what is being said. These signs may also communicate that the listener does not trust or respect the speaker. These behaviors can quickly sabotage discussions or negotiations.

In contrast, active listeners use a variety of ways to show that they are paying attention. They may nod or give verbal prompts to show they understand. They will make eye contact, but also look away every once in a while. (Research indicates that too much eye contact seems threatening and will make a person nervous.) When mediating or negotiating a conflict, paraphrasing is also a useful communication tool. When paraphrasing, the listener restates what the speaker has said, using different words. Johnson and Johnson describe this technique and its value:

> Paraphrasing improves communication. When you are restating, you cannot judge or evaluate. Restating also gives the other person direct feedback on how well you understand the messages. If you do not fully understand, the other person can add messages until you do. If you are interpreting a message differently from the way it was intended, the other person can clarify it. Paraphrasing indicates that you want to understand what the other person is saying. It shows that you care enough to listen carefully and you take what the other person is saying seriously.

Perspective taking is another function of active listening. It involves investigating the attitudes and viewpoints of the other side. It explores the cultural and social differences that may affect how the conflict is managed. Consider an incident in which teens have egged cars along a street. What might seem like a harmless prank to them may seem like a crime to the cars' owners. The step of perspective taking is often neglected when managing conflict. Social research has found this to be a mistake. A study on conflict in schools found that not thinking about different perspectives always hurts constructive conflict resolution.

Good perspective taking allows the two sides to sort out each other's position. Even if they still disagree, the two sides can trust that they heard each other and understand where each is coming from. Active listening skills demonstrate interest and respect toward the other side. These simple actions can go a long way toward defusing conflict. Respect can lead to trust, and trust is essential for moving toward a constructive resolution.

HONEST, CONSIDERATE SPEECH

Sorting out conflict requires a dialogue, a back-and-forth discussion. This might take place as a negotiation between the people in the conflict. A mediator or arbitrator can also guide the talks.

Presenting one's side in a dispute requires a balancing act. It takes an honest sharing of concerns, reasons, and feelings. At the same time it involves consideration for the other side's concerns, reasons, and feelings. Statements should not be aggressive. They should not be passive. This is not easy. It often requires two sides in a dispute inching toward trusting each other.

Blaming or accusing someone is a solid way to escalate a conflict. When people feel attacked, their first reaction is usually to defend themselves or to counterattack. No one likes to be accused or told that he or she is wrong. Psychologists have found that using "I" statements instead of "you" statements can help keep conflicts from escalating. "I" statements are communications that begin with "I feel . . ." or "I think . . ." They effectively communicate feelings and thoughts. This approach avoids ignoring the other side's feelings, blaming them for what happened, or faulting them for disagreeing.

Heidi Burgess, founder and co-director of the University of Colorado Conflict Information Consortium, compares the effects of "I" messages and "you" messages this way: "[I]f you say, 'I felt let down,' rather than, 'You broke your promise,' you will convey the same information. But you will do so in a way that is less likely to provoke a defensive or hostile reaction from your opponent."

"You" messages encourage the recipient to deny wrong-doing or to blame back. For example, if you say, "You broke your promise," the answer is likely to be, "No, I didn't," which sets people up for a lengthy argument, or, "Well, you did, too," which also continues the conflict.

"I" messages simply state a problem, without blaming someone for it. This makes it easier for the other side to help solve the problem, without having to admit that they were wrong.

There is a downside to "I" statements that must be noted. A person might use them to try to make someone else do something. "I feel bad when you . . ." can become a guilt trip to try to control another person's behavior. This betrays trust and weakens relationships.

LEARNING THE CONFLICT RESOLUTION TANGO

Emotional awareness and self-control. Active listening and perspective taking. Honest, considerate speech. These skills and behaviors are valuable even if a person never experiences a dispute. Mastery of them will make her or him a great person to be around. They will bring more confidence, sensitivity, and courage to their relationships. However, life without conflict is neither likely nor desirable. As noted earlier, constructive conflict contributes to personal growth. It is also needed to keep people and organizations honest.

Over time, conflict resolution professionals and scholars have outlined effective steps in the conflict resolution process. Of course, every dispute is different. Following a structure, though, keeps a negotiation or mediation from losing its focus. It also assures participants that they are being treated fairly.

Here is an example of a 10-step negotiation or mediation process:

1. Both sides confirm that they have their emotions under control. If that is not the case, the negotiation should be postponed.
2. Each side agrees that it desires a constructive resolution and will work together to try to create it. Each side agrees to follow the rules guiding the negotiation—no insults, no interruptions, etc.
3. Each side takes turns describing its understanding of the issue and what it wants now. Without judging or criticizing, the other side paraphrases what it hears.
4. Each side takes turns describing how it feels. Without judging or criticizing, the other side paraphrases what it hears.
5. Both sides express reasons for what they want and feel.
6. Each side expresses its understanding of the other side's perspective.
7. The two sides work together to brainstorm multiple options that benefit them both.
8. Both sides discuss which options are realistic and that they believe they can agree to and honor.
9. Both sides agree on a course of action, write it out, and sign it. A resolution should be specific in detailing what each side is expected to do. Both sides should walk away feeling that the deal is fair and workable.

10. After a week or so, the two sides meet again to see if the resolution is working. If one or both sides feel it is not, they can modify it, or agree to come up with a different plan.

Good conflict resolution skills—self-control, active listening, and considerate communication—need to be used throughout this whole process. If a participant slips into bad habits, the mediator or other person in the dispute should gently remind her or him of the rules for good conflict management.

Conflict resolution experts Roger Fisher and William L. Ury also stress the need to "separate people from the problem." The people in a conflict should not focus on who is right or wrong, or if the other side is trustworthy. Instead, they should try to concentrate on the specific behaviors or actions that are at the root of the conflict.

In a good conflict resolution process, the two sides will eventually let go of their original anger. They will become like teammates solving a problem together. That may seem to be a lot to ask when the conflict has been intense or angry. But a "work together" attitude results in the most constructive, long-lasting resolutions.

Like learning a new dance, following steps for managing conflict resolution may seem awkward at first. After a while, though, the process becomes easier. Good habits of conflict resolution management often spread to others as well. For example, schools with mediation and conflict resolution programs all report a decline in the number of disputes among students. They also describe increased cooperation throughout the school.

CREATING "WIN-WIN" RESOLUTIONS

How do two people in a conflict know if they have reached a good resolution to their problem? First, they should leave the negotiation feeling that their main concerns were addressed.

After that, they must judge if the agreement works over time. If it does not, then they should ask the other side to join them in revisiting the agreement.

Fisher and Ury suggest that any agreement should hold up to at least one of four tests:

* Do both sides have an equal chance of benefiting?
* Is the agreement fair? The two sides might test this by listing the pluses and minuses of each proposed resolution.
* Have similar agreements worked for others?
* Does the agreement benefit the wider community? Does it take care of the people most in need?

At the same time, some suggested solutions might be deal breakers. A proposal should be rejected if:

* It is illegal
* It is inappropriate
* It will hurt others
* One side believes it will not be able to keep its side of the bargain
* If it doesn't feel right, even if the reason is not clear
* If one side changes its mind

The goal, of course, is to reach an agreement where both sides "win." These win-win agreements bring about resolutions that can stand up over time. Chances are that a conflict with a "win-lose" resolution will return—sooner or later—for a rematch.

Sometimes the two sides in a conflict cannot reach a win-win resolution in their own negotiations. At that point, they should seek outside help. This may take the form of a mediator to help the two sides communicate more effectively. Another option may be an arbitrator who will listen to both sides and then make a decision that both sides agree to follow. Negotiation, mediation, and arbitration are all valuable ways to achieve constructive resolutions to conflict.

MANAGING CONFLICT IN THE JUNGLE

Everyone knows the anxiety and discomfort that follows a fight. There is also the relief that wells up when a conflict is resolved. This is even true for chimpanzees. Among animals, chimps are humans' closest relatives. Like humans, they are social animals that rely heavily on their community groups.

Recently, primatologists have focused their research on how these apes deal with conflict. They have observed some remarkable behaviors. After two chimps have a fight, they will usually ignore each other, notes primatologist Frans de Waal. They will sit near each other but will not interact or make eye contact. This disharmony ripples through the group and makes others uncomfortable. The other chimps know something is wrong.

Sometimes a third chimpanzee will try to make one of the opponents feel better with a hug or a kiss. This seems to help reduce tensions. Sometimes, de Waal says, a chimp mediator steps into the dispute. He explains that the older female may groom the male for a while, and then get up and walk very slowly to the other male. The first male will then walk right behind her so he doesn't need to make eye contact with the opponent. "And if he doesn't walk, we have seen females turn around and grab his arm and make him walk. . . ," says de Waal. "Then she may groom the other male; the three of them sit together; and then after a while she leaves and the two males continue grooming. She has brought the two parties together."

The need to repair relationships seems to be built into people, too. Even very young children will try to comfort their parents if there has been a fight.

MOVING AHEAD WITH CONFLICT RESOLUTION

Learning how to resolve conflicts constructively is a powerful skill. Instead of relying on an adult or other authority to solve problems, a person with conflict resolution skills can create his or her own solutions. It is an expression of independence, maturity, self-confidence, and even wisdom. It is a mark of sophistication and very strong character.

Mastering good conflict resolution skills takes time and practice. Good basketball players do not learn to shoot hoops in a day. A person playing chess for the first time will be lucky to learn the moves of each piece. A computer wizard with a new game will find it tough to get through the first level on the first try.

Learning how to manage conflict resolution is no different. Whether a person is in a personal dispute, mediating one, or is a jet-setting diplomat, it takes years of practice to feel comfortable with the process. It can require courage in the face of hurt feelings, hot tempers, and high stakes. Most importantly, managing conflict resolution takes the determination to pursue harmony, fair deals, and justice. It involves making compromises when it is best to do so and standing firm when necessary. Effective communication lies at the heart of all of this.

Conflict, violence, and wars may dominate the news and make the world seem like a crazy place. Bringing peace out of conflict remains humanity's greatest source of hope. It may be the most honorable purpose in the world.

GLOSSARY

active listening Technique for letting a speaker know that a listener is paying attention

adversarial system Legal process in which two sides argue against each other

aggression Hostile action, attack, or threatening behavior

anthropology Study of human development and culture

arbitration Conflict resolution strategy that features a third party to judge the dispute and provide a course of action

assertive Expressing wants and needs in a confident and respectful way

compromise A settlement in which the sides agree to accept less than what they originally wanted in order to end a dispute

constructive conflict Dispute that leads to an improvement or positive development

containment Strategy for keeping a conflict from growing worse

destructive conflict Dispute that has turned abusive or violent

diplomacy Official communications and negotiations, usually between countries

escalate Make a conflict worse

extremist Person who holds radical, severe beliefs

genocide The attempt to kill everyone within an ethnic, racial, or religious group

interpersonal Involving relationships between people

intervene Get involved to change what is happening

intimidate Use fear to try to make someone obey

intractable conflict Angry dispute, often with a long history, that is difficult to resolve

mediation Conflict resolution strategy that features a third party to help guide and referee the negotiation

nonviolent protest   Peaceful confrontation with the intent of causing change

paraphrase   Repeat back a speaker's statements in the listener's own words

passive   Not taking action

perspective taking   Asking questions and doing research to understand the other side in a conflict

psychology   Study of human thinking and behavior

self-esteem   Confidence in one's identity and abilities

sociology   Study of human and group behavior in society

BIBLIOGRAPHY

American Psychological Association. "Review of research shows that playing violent video games can heighten aggression." *APA Online*, April 19, 2005. Available online. URL: http://www.apa.org/releases/violentvideoC05.html. Accessed September 1, 2008.

American Psychological Association. *Love Doesn't Have to Hurt.* Pamphlet available online at http://www.apa.org/pi/cyf/teen.pdf. Accessed September 1, 2008.

BBC News Channel. "Rwanda: How the genocide happened." April 1, 2004. Available online. URL: http://news.bbc.co.uk/1/hi/world/africa/1288230.stm. Accessed September 1, 2008.

Binder, Brad. "Psychosocial benefits of the martial arts: Myth or reality? A literature review." Available online. URL: http://userpages.chorus.net/wrassoc/articles/psychsoc.htm. Accessed September 1, 2008.

Brown, Dee. *Bury My Heart at Wounded Knee: An Indian History of the American West.* New York: Henry Holt and Company, 1991.

Burgess, Heidi. "I-Messages and You-Messages." BeyondIntractability.org, October 2003. Available online. URL: www.beyondintractability.org/essay/I-messages. Accessed September 1, 2008.

Cauchon, Dennis. "Zero-tolerance policies lack flexibility." *USA Today,* April 13, 1999. Available online. URL: http://www.usatoday.com/educate/ednews3.htm. Accessed September 1, 2008.

Chamberlain, S.P. "An interview with . . . Susan Limber and Sylvia Cedillo: Responding to bullying." *Intervention in School and Clinic* 38, no. 4 (2003): 236–242.

Chigas, Diana. "Track II (Citizen) Diplomacy." Beyond Intractability, Conflict Information Consortium, University of Colorado, Boulder, August 2003. Available online. URL:

http://www.beyondintractability.org/essay/track2_diplomacy. Accessed September 1, 2008.

Cummings, E. Mark, and Patrick Davies. *Children and Marital Conflict: The Impact of Family Dispute and Resolution.* New York: The Guilford Press, 1994.

Deutsch, Morton, and Peter T. Coleman, eds. *The Handbook of Conflict Resolution.* San Francisco: Jossey-Bass, 2004.

Deutsch, Morton. *The Resolution of Conflict.* New Haven, Conn.: Yale University Press, 1973.

Diamond, Louisa. "Multi-Track Diplomacy in the 21st Century." People Building Peace. Available online. URL: http://www.gppac.net/documents/pbp_f/part1/6_multit.htm. Accessed September 1, 2008.

Fisher, Erik A., and Steven W. Sharp. *The Art of Managing Everyday Conflict.* London: Praeger, 2004.

Flecknoe, Mervyn. "What does anyone know about peer mediation?" *Improving Schools* 8 no. 3, (November 2005): 221–235.

Fox, James Alan, et al. *Bullying Prevention is Crime Prevention.* Pamphlet available online. URL: http://www.fightcrime.org/reports/BullyingReport.pdf. Accessed September 1, 2008.

Giraffe Heroes Project. "A Giraffe has been sighted in CA." Available online. URL: http://www.giraffe.org/hero_Kaneesha.html. Accessed September 1, 2008.

Giraffe Heroes Project. "A Giraffe has been sighted in WA." Available online. URL: http://www.giraffe.org/hero_Swagart.htm. Accessed September 1, 2008.

Gurian, Anita, and Alice Pope. "Do kids need friends?" New York University Child Study Center; excerpted in *Social and Interpersonal Problems Related to School-Age Youth.* Available online at http://smhp.psych.ucla.edu/pdfdocs/social-Problems/socialprobs.pdf. Accessed September 1, 2008.

Hair, Elizabeth C., Justin Jager, and Sarah B. Garrett. "Helping teens develop healthy social skills and relationships: What the research shows about navigating adolescence." *Trends Research Brief,* July 2002. Available online. URL: http://

www.childtrends.org/Files//Child_Trends-2002_07_01_RB_
TeenSocialSkills.pdf. Accessed September 1, 2008.

Harris, Sandra, and Conley Hathorn. "Texas middle school principals' perceptions of bullying on campus." *NASSP Bulletin*
90, no.1 (March 2006): 49–67.

Hershberg, Jim. "Anatomy of a Controversy." *The Cold War International History Project Bulletin* 5 (Spring 1995). Available
online. URL: www.gwu.edu/~nsarchiv/nsa/cuba_mis_cri/
moment.htm. Accessed September 1, 2008.

InfoUSA, U.S. Department of State, "Gideon v. Wainwright
(1963)." Available online at http://usinfo.state.gov/infousa/
government/overview/67.html. Accessed September 1,
2008.

Johnson, David W., and Roger T. Johnson. *Reducing School Violence Through Conflict Resolution.* Alexandria, Va.: Association for Supervision and Curriculum Development, 1995.

Kemple, Kristen M. "Understanding and facilitating preschool
children's peer acceptance." Available online. URL: http://
www.ed.gov/databases/ERIC_Digests/ed345866.html.
Accessed September 1, 2008.

Kopkind, Andrew. "The Grape Pickers' Strike." *The New Republic,* January 29, 1966, 12–15.

Kotlowitz, Alex. "Blocking the Transmission of Violence."
The New York Times, May 4, 2008, 5. Available online.
URL: http://www.nytimes.com/2008/05/04/magazine/
04health-t.html?hp=&pagewanted=print. Accessed
September 1, 2008.

Lefer, Diane. "Both sides: Connie Rice lays down the law to
cops and gangs." *The Sun,* April 2008, 4–11.

Lincoln, Abraham. First Inaugural Address, available online.
URL: http://www.bartleby.com/124/pres31.html. Accessed
September 1, 2008.

Liptak, Adam. "County Says It's Too Poor to Defend the Poor."
The New York Times, April 15, 2003. Available online. URL:
http://query.nytimes.com/gst/fullpage.html?res=9C05E7D

D113BF936A25757C0A9659C8B63. Accessed September 1, 2008.

McGuire, Terry. "Conflict resolution: Peer mediators guide fellow students." *The Catholic Northwest Progress,* April 1, 2004. Available online at the Conflict Resolution Unlimited Web site. URL: http://www.cruinstitute.org/articles/ CNWP-01.html. Accessed September 1, 2008.

Milburn, Tom M. "What can we learn from comparing mediation across levels." Available online. URL: http://www.gmu. edu/academic/pcs/milburn.htm. Accessed September 1, 2008.

Molidor, C., R.M. Tolman, and J.K. Kober. "Gender and contextual factors in adolescent dating violence." *Prevention Researcher* 7 (2000): 1–4.

Morse, Philip S., and Allen E. Ivey. *Face to Face: Communication and Conflict Resolution in the Schools.* Thousand Oaks, Calif.: Corwin Press.

PBS Online. "Not in our town I: The original story." Available online. URL: http://www.pbs.org/niot/about/niot1.html. Accessed September 1, 2008.

Rackove, Jack N. *James Madison and the Creation of the American Republic.* Glenview, Ill.: Scott, Foresman/Little Brown Higher Education, 1990.

Sack, Kevin. "Doctors say 'I'm sorry' before 'See you in court.'" *The New York Times,* May 18, 2008.

Salter, Jim. "Small-time Hannibal criminal had a big impact on the law." Associated Press Newswires, March 15, 2003. Available online. URL: www.nacdl.org/public.nsf/Printer-Friendly/news01?openDocument. Accessed September 1, 2008.

Schellenberg, James A. *Conflict Resolution: Theory, Research, and Practice.* Albany: State University of New York Press, 1996.

Schneider, Carl D. "What It Means To Be Sorry: The Power Of Apology In Mediation." *Mediation Quarterly* 17, no. 3 (Spring

2000). Available online. URL: http://www.mediationmatters. com/Resources/apology.htm. Accessed September 1, 2008.

Small, Fred. "Not in Our Town." Available online. URL: http:// www.jg.org/folk/artists/fredsmall/not.in.our.town.lyrics. html. Accessed September 1, 2008.

Sofia News Agency/novinite.com. "Australia apologized officially to Aborigines." Available online. URL: http://www. novinite.com/view_news.php?id=90340. Accessed September 1, 2008.

Stalinsky, Steven. "Televised Hate Speech from the Mosques." Teach Kids Peace. Available online. URL: http:// www.teachkidspeace.org/doc142.php. Accessed September 1, 2008.

Streisand, Barbara. "Speech at the John F. Kennedy School of Government, February 3, 1995." *In Our Own Words: Extraordinary Speeches of the American Century,* edited by Robert G. Torricelli and Andrew Carroll, 409. New York: Kodansha International, 1999.

Sydney Morning Herald. "Frail egos caught in killer net," December 1, 2007. Available online. URL: http://www. smh.com.au/cgi-bin/common/popupPrintArticle.pl?path= /articles/2007/11/30/1196394619060.html. Accessed September 1, 2008.

Tejada-Flores, Rick. "Cesar Chavez & the UFW." *Oxford Encyclopedia of Latinos and Latinas in the United States*, 2004. Available online. URL: http://www.pbs.org/itvs/fightfields/ cesarchavez.html. Accessed September 1, 2008.

Ury, William L. "Conflict Resolution among the Bushmen: Lessons in Dispute Systems Design." *Negotiation Journal* 11, no. 4 (October 1995): 379–389.

Ury, William L., ed. *Must We Fight?* San Francisco: Jossey-Bass, 2002.

Ury, William L. "Third Siders." BeyondIntractability.org, 2003. Available online. URL: www.beyondintractability.org/essay/ Thirdsiders/?nid=1111. Accessed September 1, 2008.

Vossekuil, B., et al. *The final report and findings of The Safe School Initiative: Implications for the prevention of school attacks in the United States*, 2002. Available online. URL: http://modelprograms.samh-sa.gov/pdfs/FactSheets/ Olweus%20Bully.pdf. Accessed September 1, 2008.

Webster-Doyle, Dr. T. "A.R.M. Your Students With Knowledge." Available online. URL: http://www.martialartsforpeace. com/pages/entermap.html#Anchor-What-16916. Accessed September 1, 2008.

Young, Steve. "A broken treaty haunts the Black Hills." *Argus Leader,* June 27, 2001. Available online. URL: http://www. bluecloud.org/bighorn-4.html. Accessed September 1, 2008.

FURTHER RESOURCES

Bodnarchuk, Kari J. *Rwanda: A Country Torn Apart.* Minneapolis, Minn.: Lerner Publishing Group, 1999.

Casey, Carolyn. *Conflict Resolution: The Win-Win Solution.* Berkeley Heights, N.J.: Enslow Publishers, 2001.

Friedman, Laurie S. *The Middle East.* Introducing Issues With Opposing Viewpoints. Farmington Hills, Mich.: Greenhaven Press, 2007.

Lewis, Barbara A. *What Do You Stand For?* Minneapolis, Minn.: Free Spirit Publishing, 2005.

Meltzer, Milton. *Ain't Gonna Study War No More.* New York: Random House, 2002.

Packer, Alex J. *The How Rude! Handbook Of Family Manners For Teens: Avoiding Strife in Family Life.* Minneapolis, Minn.: Free Spirit Publishing, 2004.

Sheehan, J. Kevin. *A Leader Becomes a Leader: Inspirational Stories of Leadership for a New Generation.* Belmont, Mass.: True Gifts Publishing, 2007.

WEB SITES

Stop Bullying Now
www.stopbullyingnow.hrsa.gov
This Web site provides information and resources to help both bullies and their victims understand and deal with the problem of bullying.

The Giraffe Heroes Project
www.giraffe.org
The Giraffe Heroes Project honors those who "stick their necks out" for the common good. The project's site features stories about brave people and peacemakers who are making a difference in their communities.

GirlsHealth.gov

www.girlshealth.gov

This government Web site offers health and relationship advice for teen girls and young women.

National Youth Violence Prevention Resource Center

www.safeyouth.org

This government Web site provides a wide range of resources for stopping violence by and against young people.

Students Against Violence Everywhere

www.nationalsave.org

SAVE shares stories about young people who are managing conflict, and provides ideas on how youth can make their communities safer.

Seeds of Peace

www.seedsofpeace.org

This organization brings together youth of different religions, races, and nationalities and helps them forge new strategies for addressing conflict, hate, and violence.

PICTURE CREDITS

INDEX

D

Dallaire, Roméo, 100–102
Dartmouth Indians/Princeton
    Tigers, 23
Das Gupta, Tapas K., 106
dating
    abuse and, 46
    conflict and, 44, 45
    friendship and, 42
Dayan, Moshe, 92
de Waal, Frans, 116
deal breakers, 115
Delano, California, 80–82, 83
Delano grape strike, 80–82
deliberate discourse, 21
Democratic Party, 82, 86
    Democratic National
        Convention, 89
    Northern Democrats, 91
    Southern Democrats, 87, 91
demonizing of other side, 19–20
Depression, the, 91
destructive conflict, 17, 18–21, 104
    developments leading to, 90
    in home environment, 29
    traits of, 18, 19, 20
    U.S. Civil War as, 84–88, 89,
        90–91
Deutsch, Morton, 18, 53, 89, 90
diplomacy
    globalization and, 97–98
    preventive diplomacy, 98,
        100–102
Doyle, Dr. Webster T., 43

E

Early Childhood Social-Emotional
    Learning (ECSEL) curriculum,
    35–36
economic conflict/labor disputes,
    80–82
emotional abuse. *See* abuse
emotional awareness, 108–109
environmental issues
    Nature Conservancy and,
        22–23
    resources, conflict and,
        67–68
"essential virtues," 17
ethnic conflict, 100–102
evasive conflict management style,
    34
Executive branch, U.S.
    government, 76

extremists, 96–97. *See also*
    terrorism

F

*Face to Face: Communication and
    Conflict Resolution in the Schools*
    (Morse and Ivey), 56
FaceBook, 44
Family Circle bullying survey, 50
family conflict, 29, 30–33
    constructive conflict and,
        32–33
    destructive conflict and,
        31–32
    main forms of, 31
    role models and, 31
    young children, effect on, 29
    See also home environment
farm workers' strike/boycott,
    80–82
feelings. *See* emotional awareness
Fight Crime: Invest in Kids
    (organization), 50
Finding Nemo (movie), 37–38
Fisher, Erik A., 28, 35
Fisher, Roger, 114, 115
Flecknoe, Mervyn, 48, 56
football game, selective perception
    and, 23
forms of conflict, 13–26
Fort Laramie Treaty of 1868, 20–21
Fort Scott, Kansas, 85
friendship, 37–46
    conflicts and, 38
    importance of, 38
    peer pressure and, 39
    resolution of conflicts and,
        39–42

G

Gandhi, Mohandas (Mahatma),
    88, 89
gang warfare, 69–70, 71
Gates, Robert, 26
genocide, 92
George III (king), 74
Gideon, Clarence Earl, 77–79
Gideon v. Wainwright decision, 78
Giraffe Heroes Project, 48
Global Negotiation Project, 63
globalization
    defined, 97
    diplomacy and, 97–98
Godefroy, Christian H., 37

ABOUT THE AUTHOR
AND CONSULTANTS

Sean McCollum has published more than 20 nonfiction books and hundreds of magazine articles for children and teens. He is a regular contributor to *National Geographic Kids, Scholastic Choices, Cousteau Kids,* and other youth publications. He hikes, bikes, and climbs mountains near Boulder, Colorado. To find out more about his books, visit his Web site at www.kidfreelance.com.

Series consultant **Dr. Madonna Murphy** is a professor of education at the University of St. Francis in Joliet, Illinois, where she teaches education and character education courses to teachers. She is the author of *Character Education in America's Blue Ribbon Schools, First & Second Edition* and *History & Philosophy of Education: Voices of Educational Pioneers.* She has served as the character education consultant for a series of more than 40 character education books for elementary school children, on the Character Education Partnership's Blue Ribbon Award committee recognizing K-12 schools for their character education, and on a national committee for promoting character education in teacher education institutions.

Series consultant **Sharon L. Banas** was a middle school teacher in Amherst, New York, for more than 30 years. She led the Sweet Home Central School District in the development of its nationally acclaimed character education program. In 1992, Banas was a member of the Aspen Conference, drafting the Aspen Declaration that was approved by the U.S. Congress. In 2001, she published *Caring Messages for the School Year.* Banas has been married to her husband, Doug, for 37 years. They have a daughter, son, and new granddaughter.